CW01507461

LLANDEILO TO SWANSEA

Including the Llanelli and Carmarthen Branches

John Organ

MP Middleton Press

Front Cover: Pontarddulais was formerly an important junction, where the Swansea and Llanelli lines diverged, which embraced an extensive station complex. Class 5MT 4-6-0 no. 73025 was viewed as it departed from the main line up platform with a train from Swansea to Shrewsbury in 1962. (D.Johnson/R.S.Carpenter coll.)

Rear Cover: Since the closure of Swansea Victoria and the former LNWR route south of Pontarddulais, the "Heart of Wales" services now terminate at the former GWR Swansea High Street Station. DMU no.153 327 awaits departure to Shrewsbury via Llanelli, whilst alongside no. D1015 Western Champion *has just arrived with a special train from Paddington on 15th June 2002. (P.G.Barnes)*

Published February 2009

ISBN 978 1 906008 46 8

© *Middleton Press, 2009*

Design Deborah Esher
Typesetting Barbara Mitchell

Published by
        Middleton Press
        Easebourne Lane
        Midhurst
        West Sussex
        GU29 9AZ
Tel: 01730 813169
Fax: 01730 812601
Email: info@middletonpress.co.uk
www.middletonpress.co.uk

Printed & bound by MPG Biddles Ltd, Kings Lynn

INDEX

We use the original spellings for Llanelly (Llanelli since 1966), Llandilo (Llandeilo since 1971) and Pontardulais (Pontarddulais since 1971) in relation to the periods referred to in the text. The current names are used as section headings. Many locations throughout Wales had their traditional and historic names changed to a version more applicable to the Welsh language.

ACKNOWLEDGEMENTS

I am once again very grateful for the assistance received from the many photographers and collectors mentioned in the credits. In addition I must also thank G.Croughton, J.Fozard, S.Jenkins (LOSA), N.Langridge, N.Nicholson (WRRC), B.Pearce, Mr D. and Dr S.Salter, N.W.Sprinks and T.Walsh (LOSA), who have all made an invaluable contribution. Finally I must once again add a special word of thanks to my wife Brenda who has provided much tolerance and support during the period of research and compilation.

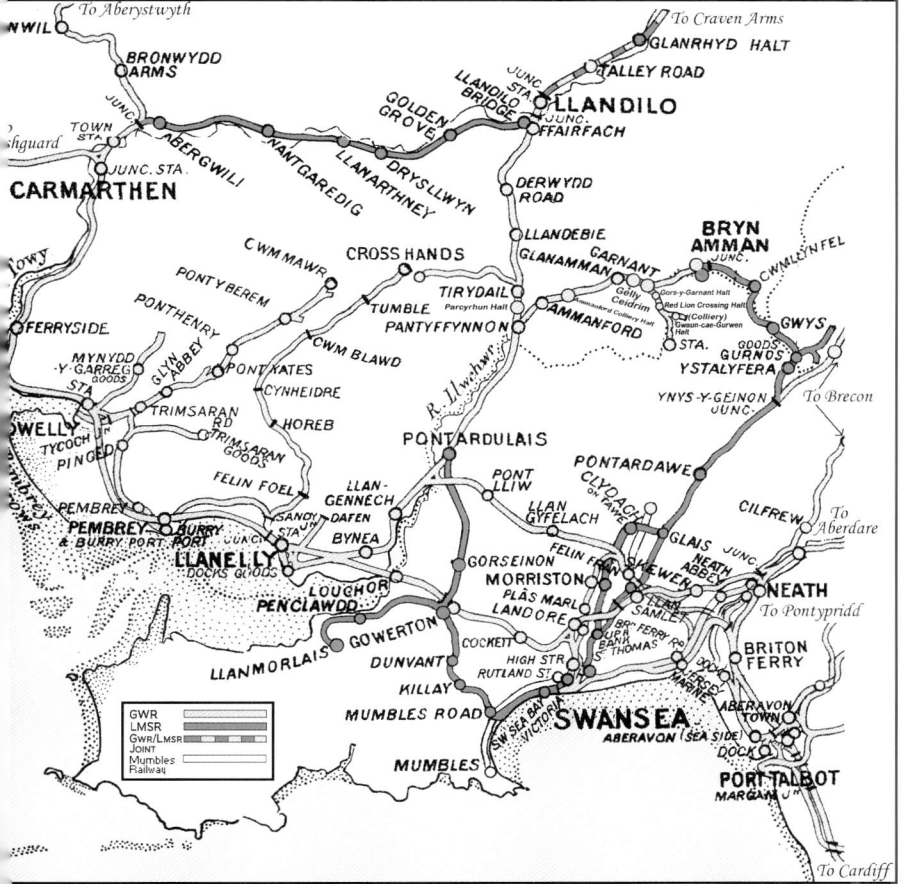

I. Railway Clearing House map, with minor alterations, including the routes covered in this volume and their former ownership.

GEOGRAPHICAL SETTING

Our journey commences at Llandeilo, which was once the largest intermediate station on the Central Wales Line between Craven Arms and Swansea. Immediately to the south of the station, the Carmarthen Branch diverged to the west at the beginning of its 13 mile journey through a sparsely inhabited rural area, following the River Towy to Abergwili Junction, a short distance to the north of the county town.

Returning to the main line, the route adopts a southerly course, spanning the River Towy and passing the minor station at Ffairfach before climbing through a wooded valley of the River Cennen on a rising gradient for two miles at 1 in 105. The summit at 230ft is reached at Derwydd, five miles from Llandeilo. The line now leaves the rural surroundings and enters the western extremities of the, now largely abandoned, mining and industrial regions in the valleys of the Rivers Marlais and Amman. Spoil heaps and pits were once visible whilst a number of industrial and mining lines branched away on both sides of the route between Llandybie and Ammanford, formerly named Tirydail. One of these lines was the fabled Great Western Railway Mountain Branch, a short steeply graded line that originally used rope haulage. This line provided access to the Great Mountain Collieries at Tumble, near Cross Hands. The major junction at Pantyffynnon is reached after a further five miles. Here the GWR Brynamman Branch connected with the Central Wales Line from a northeasterly direction. This heavily graded six mile long largely freight line had an end-on connection with an isolated branch of the Midland Railway at its eastern terminus. The GWR branch line, which incorporated another short branch from Glanamman to Gwaun-cae-Gurwen, was the source of much of the coal traffic carried over the Central Wales Line.

After a five mile long stretch of formerly double track, another junction was approached at Pontarddulais. Here the Llanelli Branch veered off to the southwest, whilst the principal route towards Swansea proceeded on its southerly course. After leaving Pontarddulais, the route passed under another GWR line, which was part of the Swansea District Line. The surroundings in this area had been devastated by huge open cast mining operations around Grovesend, whilst further pits and spoil heaps were passed as the line descended to Gorseinon, 17 miles from Llandeilo. Following a short stretch of level track, the line climbed to cross the GWR main line linking London with West Wales at Gowerton, followed by an ascent at 1 in 70 to Dunvant. The former LNWR station at Gowerton South was the location of a junction with a freight only branch line to Llanmorlais. There then followed a descent on curving gradients of 1 in 80 through Killay and Cline Woods towards Swansea Bay, until the coast was reached at Mumbles Road Station, 23 miles from Llandeilo.

The Swansea & Mumbles Railway, also known as the Oystermouth Railway, was crossed a short distance beyond Mumbles Road after which the Central Wales Line followed the coast through Swansea Bay station and St.Helens before veering inland. The route climbed briefly before passing the depot at Paxton Street, after which a curving descent at 1 in 45 led to the terminal station at Swansea Victoria, 26 miles from Llandeilo.

Retracing our journey to Pontarddulais, the former Llanelli Branch proceeds to the southwest along a single track formation. After passing through a short tunnel with limited clearance, the Lougher Estuary is visible to the east together with distant views of the Gower Peninsular. The surrounding area is marshy and low lying with more evidence of the once flourishing mining industry, which in recent years has suffered a severe decline. Two miles south of Pontarddulais, a triangular junction known as Hendy and Morlais Junctions connects the Llanelli line to the former GWR Swansea District Line. This was constructed in 1913 to allow freight traffic direct access to the industrial heartland of South Wales in the Cardiff and Newport areas by avoiding the congested layout in central Swansea. Prior to the rationalisation after 1964, Morlais Junction originally featured a "flying junction" whereby the up GWR route branched away from the CWL up line and crossed above the down line of our route. Two minor stations at Llangennech and Bynea are encountered before the Central Wales Line completes its independent route through Wales.

Shortly after passing Bynea, the Central Wales route joins the former GWR main line at Llandeilo Junction, five miles from Pontarddulais. The remaining two miles of the journey to Llanelli are shared with the line from London to Fishguard. Originally the route of the predecessor of the Central Wales Line, the Llanelly Railway & Dock Company, crossed the GWR line at an oblique level crossing called Llandilo Crossing and terminated at a station known as Llanelly Dock. This level crossing of tracks remained in place until 1966.

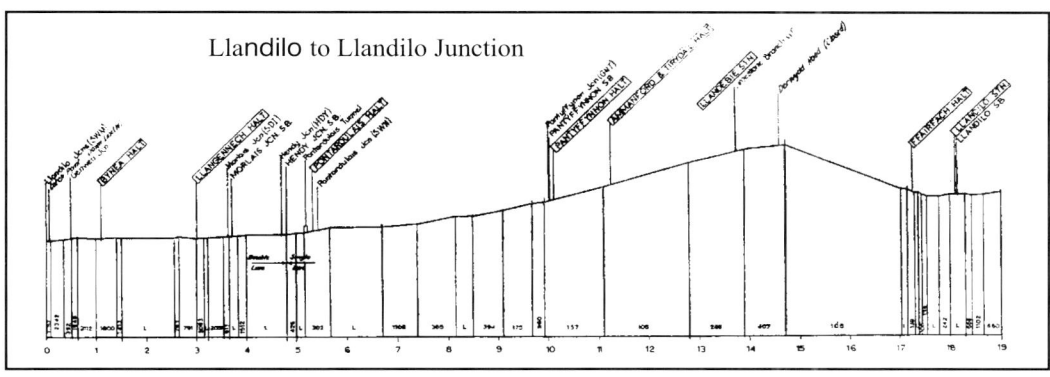

Llandilo to Llandilo Junction

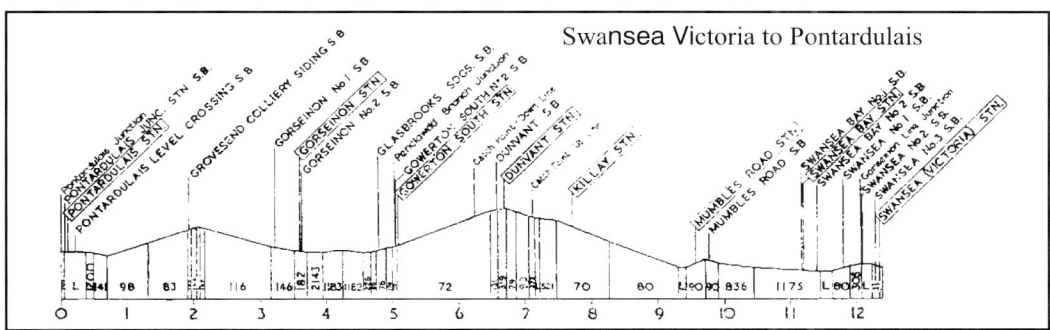

Swansea Victoria to Pontardulais

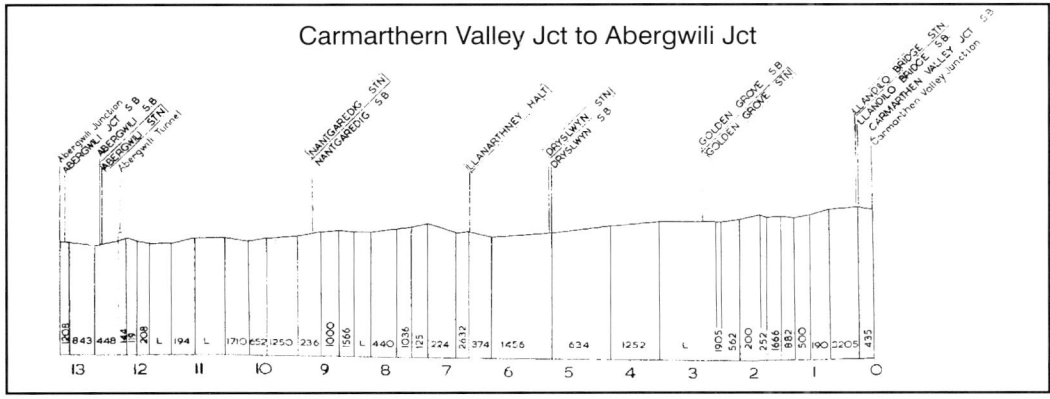

Carmarthern Valley Jct to Abergwili Jct

HISTORICAL BACKGROUND

The southern section of the Central Wales Line has a fairly complex history. The Llanelly Railroad (later renamed Railway) & Dock Company had been incorporated by an Act of Parliament dated 19th June 1828. This ultimately authorised the construction of a railway linking Llanelly and Llandilo, a distance of 17 miles. This line was opened in stages between 1839 and 1857. The first section to be built was the seven miles from Llanelly Dock to Pontardulais, followed by four miles to Pantyffynon in 1840 and a further one mile to Tirydail (formerly known as Duffryn) in 1841. The protracted construction of the entire route to Llandilo required a further sixteen years to complete, before it was finally opened throughout in 1857. When the Vale of Towy Railway opened in 1858, linking Llandilo and Llandovery, it was leased to and administered by the Llanelly Railway. With the encouragement of the London & North Western Railway, the Llanelly Railway gained powers to construct the 12 mile long line from Pontardulais to Swansea Victoria in 1861.This important link was opened for freight traffic in January 1866, but passenger services were not introduced until 14th December 1867. The LNWR took over the ownership of the line in September 1873. During the same period the LRDC also constructed the Carmarthen Branch from Llandilo to Abergwili Junction, which opened for freight in November 1864 and passengers in June 1865. This line was also taken over by the LNWR in 1873.

The Llanelly Railway was to be absorbed by the Great Western Railway in 1889, who subsequently put their individualistic stamp on the infrastructure of their section of the line. Meanwhile the LNWR, having a vested interest in the line north of Llandovery, was granted running rights over the former lines of the Llanelly company. The ultimate result was that the Central Wales Line north of Llandovery was entirely owned by the LNWR; the former Vale of Towy section between Llandovery and Llandilo was jointly controlled by the LNWR and GWR, whilst the section from Llandilo to Llanelly was owned by the GWR alone. The section between Pontardulais and Swansea became an isolated part of the LNWR, along with the Carmarthen Branch. These complex arrangements remained throughout the 1923-1947 period of LMS and GWR control, until the entire Central Wales Line was absorbed into the Western Region of British Railways in 1948.

The Pontardulais to Swansea Victoria line was closed on 13th June 1964, after which all services were diverted to Llanelli. Within two years Victoria Station had been demolished, the site being used for a car park. The Carmarthen Branch was closed to all traffic on 9th September 1963. The remainder of the Central Wales Line remains in use.

Privatisation resulted in South Wales & West operating services from 2nd March 1997. However, after reorganisation in October 2001, Wales & Borders became the franchisee. Arriva Trains Wales took over in December 2003. The line is now marketed as the "Heart of Wales Line".

The line is supported by the Heart of Wales Line Travellers' Association, which was formed in 1981 to promote the use of the railway. The association works closely with Arriva Trains Wales in their joint endeavour to encourage the service to be used. A quarterly newsletter is published, whilst special events are occasionally organised at various locations along the route. A typical example of these events was held at Llandovery in October 2008 to celebrate the 150th anniversary of the opening of the Vale of Towy Railway between Llandilo and Llandovery.

PASSENGER SERVICES

Four trains calling at all stations, weekdays only, was the basic service over all the routes. The early 1870s brought an additional train or two, which omitted some of the smaller stations. One Swansea service on Sundays had appeared by the 20th century, although there had been one between Llandovery and Carmarthen in the 1860s.

Five or six trains served the routes in most years until World War II, when only three or four were provided, with none on Sundays. The weekday frequency returned after hostilities, but Sunday trains did not. There were a few more short workings, particularly to and from Swansea Victoria on Summer Saturdays.

The cut-backs of the mid-1960s resulted in just four trains between Llandilo and Llanelli. May 1969 brought through running of all five trains to Swansea, on the present route. The number dropped to four from May 1993, but there was subsequently an improvement in the service on Sundays.

KNIGHTON, CENTRAL WALES, and LLANELLY.—London and North Western and Llanelly.

December 1870

Miles from Craven Arms	Fares from Llandovery 1 cl. s.d.	2 cl. s.d.	3 cl. s.d.	Euston Station,	mrn	mrn	aft	mrn	aft	mrn	non	Sn aft
	....	....	....	112 London ....dep	....	....	9 15	....	....	9d10	12 0	aft
	....	....	....	113 Birmingm * ,,	....	....	1030	8 0	....	1130	2 20	
	....	....	....	116 Liverpool † ,,	....	....	1115	7e15	....	11[illegible]	1250	
	....	....	....	151 Manchestr ‡ ,,	....	....	1055	7 30	....	1145	1 30	
	....	....	....	127 Hereford § ,,	....	....	mrn	9 20	....	1230	5 15	
	....	....	....	127 Shrewsbry ,,	....	....	7 0	1010	....	2 20	5 10	
				Down.	mrn	mrn	mrn	mrn	aft	aft	aft	
—				Craven Arms..dep	All 1, 2, 3 class.	* New Street. † Lime Street. ‡ London Road Station. § Barr's Court.	8 5	1110	....	2 53	6 50	e Through carriages from Liverpool to Swansea, Carmarthen, Tenby, and Pembroke Dock.
2½	....	....	....	Broome			8 12	1118	....	....	6 58	
5¼	....	....	....	Hopton Heath			8 17	1125	....	3 4	7 5	
8	....	....	....	Bucknell [teign			8 23	1133	....	3 9	7 12	
12¼	....	....	....	Knighton, for Pres-			8 33	1142	3 40	3 18	7 22	
15	....	....	....	Knucklas			8 39	1148	3 46	....	7 2[illegible]	
18¼	....	....	....	Llangunllo			8 52	12 0	4 0	....	7 42	
[illegible]	....	....	....	Llanbister Road			9 2	12 [illegible]	4 11	....	7 52	
25¼	....	....	....	Dolau			9 13	1217	4 20	....	8 3	
29¼	....	....	....	Penybont			9 19	12[illegible]	4 27	3 54	8 10	
32	....	....	....	Llandrindod (Wlls)			9 28	1235	4 37	4 3	8 20	
37½	....	....	....	Builth Road 129..			9 41	1247	4 50	4 18	8 35	
62¼	....	....	....	129 Llanidloes ar	....		....	8 40	7 30	7 30	....	
65	....	....	....	Brecon 129 ,,	....		1110	2 20	6 55	5 50	....	
	....	....	....	Builth Road ..dep	....		9 44	1250		4 19	8 36	
39¼	....	....	....	Cilmery	....		9 49	1257		....	8 41	
[illegible]	....	....	....	Garth	....		9 57	1 8		4 31	8 48	
[illegible]	....	....	....	Llangammarch	....		10 2	1 13		Mn.	8 54	
[illegible]	....	....	....	Llanwrtyd (Wells)	....		1010	1 23		4 41	9 2	
55	....	....	....	Cynghordy	....		1026	1 39		....	9 18	mail
[illegible]	....	....	....	Llandovery	....	8 5	1043	1 55	Thurs. only.	5 8	9 30	3 30
[illegible]	1 0	0 8	0 4½	Llanwrda, fr Pump-	....	8 15	1050	2 5		5 15		3 40
[illegible]	1 3	0 10	0 5½	Llangadock [saint	....	8 20	1055	2 10		5 20		3 45
[illegible]	1 6	1 2	0 7	Glanrhyd	....	8 25	11 5	2 15		Sat.		3 50
[illegible]	1 9	1 4	0 9	Talley Road	....	8 30	11 9	2 20		5 30		3 54
[illegible]	2 0	1 6	0 11	Llandilo ......arr	....	8 35	1113	2 25		5 35		4 0
	....	....	....	*Crmrthn L.* Llandilo ....dep	Sats. only.	8 41	1115	2f30	Saturdays only.	6 25		4 5
71½	2 6	2 0	1 2½	Golden Grove		8 53	1128	2 43		6 38		4 20
74½	3 0	2 6	1 6	Llanarthney		9 3	1139	2 52		6 47		4 30
78	3 6	2 9	1 8	Nantgaredig		9 8	1145	2 58		6 53		4 37
82½	4 0	3 6	2 0	Abergwilly ..[31		9 17	1155	3 10		7 5		4 48
84	4 6	3 6	2 2	Carmarthen arr		9 22	12 0	3 15		7 10		4 55
—	....	....	....	31 Llandyssil arr		....	2 40	7 0		....		
—	....	....	....	31 Cardigan (Ch.)		....	5 10	....		....		
—	....	....	....	Tenby 31 .. ,,		....	1 43	6 40		....		
—	....	....	....	31 Pembrke D. ,,		....	2 20	7 20		....		
—	....	....	....	28 New Milfrd ,,		....	1 50	6 50		....		
	....	....	....	Llandilo ......dep	Saturdays only.	8 40	1113	2 27	4 0	6 39	Thursdays and Saturdays only.	
74½	2 [illegible]	2 0	1 2½	Derwydd Road		8 55	1133	....	4 15	5 52		
75½	2 9	2 3	1 4	Llandebie		9 0	1140	2 43	4 20	5 57		
77½	3 0	2 4	1 5½	Dyffryn		9 5	1145	....	....	6 5		
78½	3 3	2 6	1 7	Pantyffynnon arr		9 10	1150	2 51	4 30	6 10		
—	....	....	....	*Grnnt B.* Pantyffynnon d		10 3	3rd cls.	3 10	4 35	6 20		
79½	....	....	....	Cross Inn		10 8		a	....	6 25		
83½	....	....	....	Garnant b		1022		3 40	....	6 40		
85½	....	....	....	Brynammn 30 a		1030		3 50	5 5	6 45		
81	....	....	....	Pantyffynnon dep		9 15	12 2	2 53	Thurs. & Sats. only.	6 13		
86½	4 0	3 0	2 0	Pontardulais ..arr		9 25	1217	3 3		6 23		
—	....	....	....	*Llanelly Branch.* Pontardulas d		9 45	1 5	3 10		6 30	5 35	
85½	4 6	3 6	2 2½	Llangennech		9 51	1 11	3 16		a	5 40	
87½	5 0	4 0	2 4	Bynea		9 57	1 17	3 22		6 42	5 45	
89½	5 6	4 0	2 6	Llanelly Docks		10 5	1 25	3 30		6 50	5 52	
90½	5 6	4 0	2 7	Llanelly 28 ar	mrn	1010	1 30	3 35		6 55	5 57	
—	....	....	....	Pontardulais..dep	8 5	9 27	1230	3 5		6 27	....	
87	4 9	3 6	2 3	Gorseinon, Loughor	8 12	9 35	1240	....		6 34	....	
88½	5 6	4 0	2 5	Gower Road 29 ,,	8 37	9 40	1245	3 18		6 38	....	
91½	5 6	4 0	2 8	Penclawdd..dep	8 30	....	....	....		....	....	
90	5 0	3 9	2 6	Dunvant	8 45	9 45	1253	....		6 43	....	
91	5 6	4 0	2 7½	Killay	8 50	9 50	1258	3 29		6 48	....	
93	5 6	4 3	2 9½	Mumbles Road	8 55	9 55	1 3	3 33		6 53	....	
95½	6 0	4 6	3 6	Swansea 27,30,31	9 0	10 0	1 10	3 40		7 0	....	

† Through carriages from Liverpool to Swansea and Carmarthen.

Victoria Street,	mrn	mrn	aft	aft	aft	aft	Sun
Swansea ......dep	d Through carriages London to Carmarthen.	9 10	12[illegible]	[illegible]	[illegible] 0	5 45	Weds. and Sats. only.
Mumbles Road		9 17	12[illegible]7	[illegible]	[illegible] 7	5 53	
Killay		9 21	1242	[illegible]	[illegible] 12	5 58	
Dunvant		9 26	....	[illegible]	[illegible] 16	6 3	
Gower Road		9 31	12[illegible]	[illegible]	[illegible] 21	6 8	
Penclawdd ..arr		....	....	....	....	6 20	
Gorseinon, fr Loghr		9 35	12[illegible]	[illegible]	[illegible]		
Pontardulais ..arr		9 42	1 3	aft	[illegible]		
Llanelly Branch. Llanelly ..dep		9 0	12 [illegible]	[illegible]	[illegible] 0	Saturdays only.	6 0
Llanelly Docks		9 3	12 3	[illegible]	[illegible] 3		a
Bynea		9 13	1213	[illegible]	[illegible] 12		a
Llangennech		9 20	1219	[illegible]	[illegible] 19		a
Pontardulas a		9 25	1225	3 0	[illegible] 25		6 25
Pontardulais..dep		9 47	1 6	Thurs & Sats. only	[illegible]		
Pantyffynnon..arr		10 0	1 16		[illegible]		
Grnnt B. Brynamman dp		8 50	....		5 [illegible]		
Garnant b		8 57	....		5 [illegible]		
Cross Inn		9 10	....		5 [illegible]		
Pantyffynnon a		9 15	....		5 50		
Pantyffynnon dep		10 5	1 18		5 51		
Dyffryn		1010	1 23		5 56		
Llandebie		1015	1 28		6 0		
Derwydd Road		1020	1 33		6 5		
Llandilo ......arr		1033	1 47		6 15		
29 New Milfrd dp		....	11 0	g Through carriages to London (Euston) and Liverpool (Lime Street). h Through carriages to Liverpool (Lime Street).	....		
31 Pembrke D. ,,		....	1030		g		
Tenby 31 .. ,,		....	1110		g		
31 Cardigan (Ch.)		....	8 0		....		
31 Llandyssil ,,	mail	....	1050		....		
Crmrthn L. Carmarthen dep	6 45	....	1 g5		4f45		7 0
Abergwilly	a	....	1 10		4 50		7 7
Nantgaredig	a	....	1 20		5 0		7 17
Llanarthney	a	....	1 25		5 7		7 25
Golden Grove	a	....	1 35		5 17		7 35
Llandilo ....arr	7 25	....	1 50		5 30		7 39
Llandilo ......dep	7 27	1039	1 55		6 20		7 55
Talley Road	....	1043	Sat.		6 25		8 0
Glanrhyd	....	1048	....		6 30		8 5
Llangadock [saint	7 43	1055	2 10		6 35		8 10
Llanwrda, fr Pump-	7 48	11 0	2 15		6 40		8 15
Llandovery.. ar	7 57	11 8	2 23		6 50		8 25
Llandovery.. dp	8 0	1110	2 25		6 53		....
Cynghordy	8 10	....	....		7 3		....
Llanwrtyd (Wells)	8 25	1134	2 49		7 19		....
Llangammarch	8 32	Mn.	....		7 27		....
Garth	8 40	1145	3 0		7 33		....
Cilmery	8 49	....	....		a		....
Builth Road 129 a	8 54	1156	3 11		7 45		....
129 Brecon ....dep	7 0	1040	1 5		6 30		....
129 Llanidloes ,,	6 50	....	1130		4 30		....
Builth Road...dep	8 55	12 0	3 12		7 46		....
Llandrindod (Wlls)	9 10	1216	3 30		8 1		....
Penybont	9 19	1225	3 40		8 10		....
Dolau	9 25	....	....		8 16		....
Llanbister Road	9 35	Ths	....		a		....
Llangunllo	9 45	....	....		8 31		....
Knucklas .... mrn	9 59	....	....		a		....
Knighton 9 40	10 6	1 0	4 17		8 52		....
Bucknell 9 50	....	1 10	4 26		9 2		....
Hopton Heath 9 58	c	1 18	4 31		9 8		....
Broome [127, 5 10 5	....	1 24	....		9 13		....
Craven Arms. 1015	1030	1 32	4 42		9 23		....
127 Hereford § ar	12 0	3 25	7 25		1055		....
127 Shrewsbury ,,	1123	2 20	5 30		10 0		....
151 Manchestr ‡ ,,	2 0	5 10	7 45		2 45		....
113 Liverpool † ,,	2 30	5 40	3 0		3 20		....
116 Birminghm * ,,	3 5	5 15	7 50		2 30		....
117 Londn (Eus.) ,,	5 15	9 15	1015		5 50		....

f Stop at Dryslwyn by signal. a Stop to take up by signal, and set down on notice being given to Guard at preceding Station. b Garnant. c Stops when required to take up. Passengers set down or taken up at Cross Keys if required. Sunday Train.

3rd class to Shrewsbury, Chester, Birkenhead, Liverpool, Warrington, Manchester, Wellington, Wolverhampton, Dudley, Wednesbury, Birmingham, and London from Pembroke Dock at 10½ mrn., Tenby at 11 10 mrn., Carmarthen at 6¾ mrn. and 1 5 aft., Llanelly at 9 mrn. and 12 noon, Swansea at 9 10 mrn. and 12 30 aft., and from Central Wales Line by 8 mrn. Train from Llandovery.

3rd class to Edinburgh and Glasgow from Carmarthen at 6 45 mrn., Llanelly at 9 mrn., and Swansea at 9 10 mrn.

3rd class to Tenby and Pembroke Dock from Liverpool at 7 15 mrn., Manchester at 7 30 mrn., Shrewsbury at 10 10 mrn.: to Carmarthen, Llanelly, and Swansea, from London at 9 mrn., Liverpool at 7 15 and 11[illegible] mrn., Manchester at 7¼ and 11½ mrn., and Shrewsbury at 10 10 mrn. and 2 20 aft.; to Central Wales Line from London at 9 mrn., Liverpool at 7 15 mrn., Manchester at 7¼ mrn., and Shrewsbury at 10 10 mrn. and 2 20 aft.

February 1936

Mls	Down.	mrn	mrn		aft	aft	aft	aft	
—	**Llandilo** ....dep.	8 0	1128	..	2 15	3 50	6 5	8 20	..
¾	Llandilo Bridge..........	8 4	1132	....	2 19	3 54	6 9	8 24	....
2¾	Golden Grove	8 11	1136	..	2 23	3 58	6 13	8 28	..
5¼	Dryslwyn	8 18	1140	....	2 28	4 2	6 17	8 33	....
6½	Llanarthney	8 23	1145	..	2 32	4 6	6 21	8 37	..
9	Nantgaredig	8 31	1149	....	2 39	4 11	6 25	8 41	....
12½	Abergwili ....[141	8 42	1155	..	2 45	4 17	6 33	8 47	..
14¼	**Carmarthen 64, 69**, arr.	8 52	12 2	....	2 54	4 24	6 42	8 56	....

Mls	Up.	mrn	mrn		aft	aft	aft	aft
—	**Carmarthen**.........dep.	6 45	1019	..	1 0	2 45	5 8	6 32
1¾	Abergwili	6 51	1025	....	1 6	2 50	5 14	6 38
5¼	Nantgaredig.............	6 58	1032	..	1 12	2 57	5 21	6 44
7¾	Llanarthney	7 3	1036	....	1 17	3 1	5 25	6 50
9	Dryslwyn	7 7	1041	..	1 21	3 6	5 30	6 54
11½	Golden Grove	7 13	1046	....	1 26	3 10	5 34	6 58
14	Llandilo Bridge	7 18	1050	..	1 30	3 15	5 39	7 3
14¼	**Llandilo 492**, *(above)* arr.	7 23	1055	....	1 35	3 20	5 43	7 8

LLANDOVERY, LLANDILO, and LLANELLY

Miles	Down	mrn	mrn	mrn	aft	aft	aft	aft	aft	aft
	Llandovery..........dep.	..	8 45	10 50	Saturdays only.	..	2 10	4 15	6 50	Saturdays only.
4	Llanwrda..............	..	8 54	11 0		..	2 18	4 23	6 58	
5¾	Llangadock............	..	9 0	11 5		..	2 23	4 28	7 4	
9½	Talley Road	..	9 8	11 13		..	2 31	4 36	7 12	
11¼	**Llandilo 493** .... arr.	..	9 12	11 17		..	2 35	4 40	7 16	
	dep.	7 45	9 17	11 20		..	2 37	4 43	7 18	
12¼	Ffairfach	7 49	9 20	11 24		..	2 45	4 46	7 22	
14¾	Derwydd Road	7 56	9 28	11 31		..	2 54	4 54	7 33	
16½	Llandebie..............	8 0	9 32	11 35	..	..	2 58	4 58	7 37	
18¾	Tirydail F §...........	8 4	9 36	11 39	1230	..	3 2	5 2	7 41	
19½	Pantyffynnon 146.......	8 12	9 43	11 45	1235	1244	3 10	5 9	7 48	10 7
24	**Pontardulais 485**.......	8 21	9 52	11 53	One cl. only.	1253	3 19	5 18	7 57	1015
26½	Llangennech	8 27	9 58	11 59		1259	3 25	5 25	8 3	1021
28¾	Bynea..................	8 32	10 3	12 4		1 3	3 29	5 30	8 7	1025
31	**Llanelly 64, 69**.......arr.	8 38	10 9	12 10		1 9	3 35	5 36	8 13	1031

Miles	Up	mrn	mrn	mrn	mrn	aft	aft	aft	aft	aft
	Llanelly ....dep.	4 50	8 20	10 0	11 15	2 10	5 0	7 35	9 55	Sats. only.
2¼	Bynea..................	4 56	8 28	10 6	11 21	2 16	5 5	7 40	10 1	
4¾	Llangennech	5 1	8 33	1011	11 26	2 21	5 10	7 45	10 8	
7	**Pontardulais 485**.......	5 8	8 39	1019	11 33	2 27	5 16	7 50	1015	
11¼	Pantyffynnon § 146......	5 18	8 49	1026	11 45	2 37	5 25	7 59	1022	1030
12¾	Tirydail F	5 24	8 55	..	11 51	2 43	5 32	8 5	Saturdays only.	1036
14¼	Llandebie..............	5 30	9 1	..	11 57	2 49	5 38	8 11		One class only.
16½	Derwydd Road	5 34	9 5	..	12 1	2 54	5 49	8 16		
18¼	Ffairfach	5 42	9 13	..	12 9	3 2	5 57	8 23		
19¾	**Llandilo 493** .... arr.	5 45	9 16	..	12 12	3 4	6 0	8 26		
	dep.	..	9 17	..	12 13	3 6	6 1	8 27		
21¾	Talley Road	..	9 22	..	12 18	3 11	6 6	8 32		
25½	Llangadock............	..	9 31	..	12 26	3 20	6 14	8 40		
27	Llanwrda..............	..	9 37	..	12 31	3 25	6 20	8 45		
31	Llandovery ....arr.	..	[illegible]	..	12 39	3 33	6 27	8 52		

F ¼ mile to Ammanford.
§ "Halt" at Parcyrhun between Tirydail and Pantyffynnon.

*** For **OTHER TRAINS** between Llandovery & Pontardulais, page 492

Dec 1938

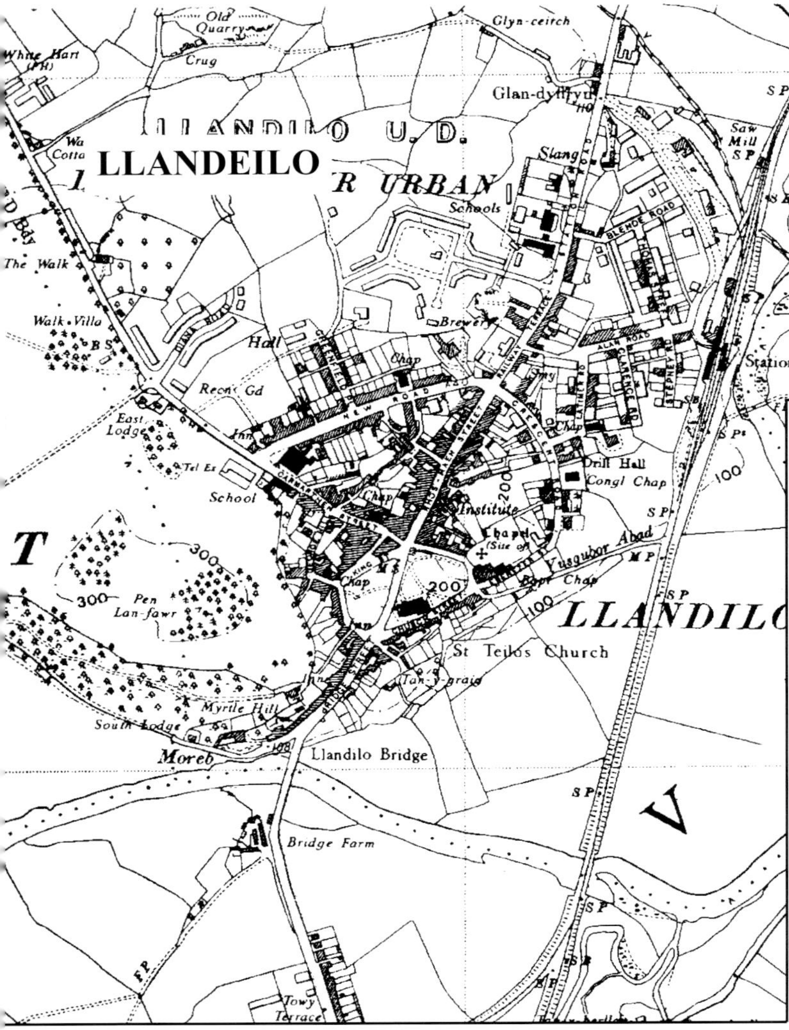

II. This was once the largest intermediate station on the Central Wales Line, which in its heyday boasted excellent passenger facilities including a refreshment room. This 1948 survey at 6ins to one mile shows the full extent of the complex plus the Carmarthen Valley Junction immediately south of the bridge across the River Towy.

1. A view of the track layout in the signal box provides a good indication of the extensive complex in 1958, when it was at its greatest extent. Along with many other towns in Wales, the traditional name of Llandilo was changed to the current Welsh version in 1971. (G.Adams/M.J.Stretton coll.)

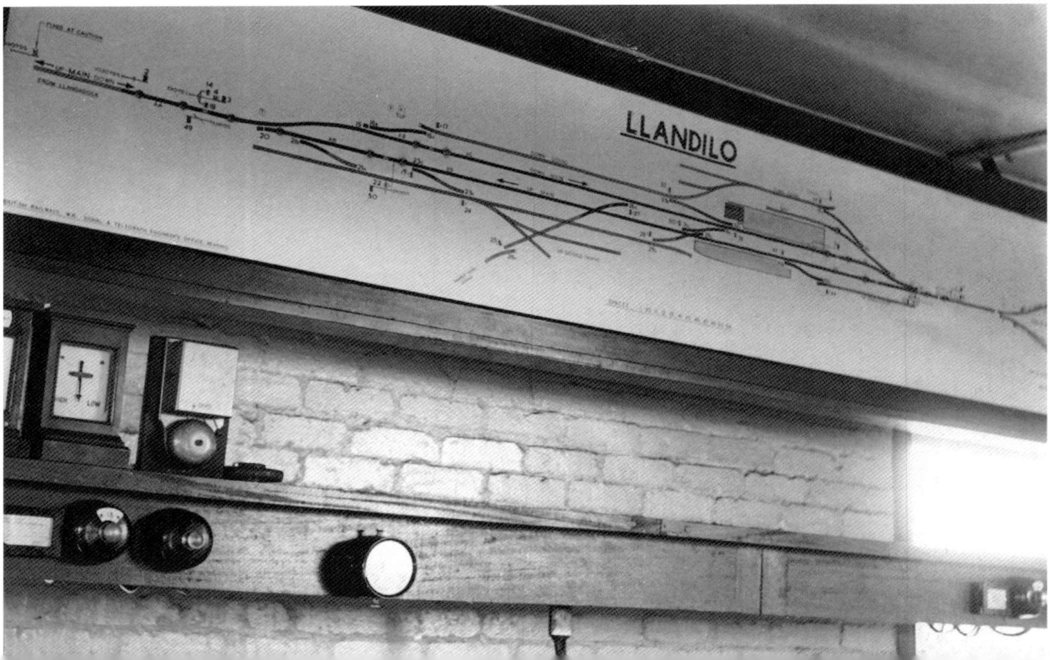

2. 0-6-0PT no.7425 was viewed in the up platform, having run around the carriages prior to shunting them to the down platform before departing with a southbound train for Llanelly on 19th March 1960. (WRRC/Stratton coll.)

3. A view of the station looking north shows the characteristic GWR style of station design to advantage. The locomotive featured in the previous photograph can be seen drawing the stock into the down platform. (WRRC/Stratton coll.)

4.   This is another view of the station from the south, taken on this occasion from the up platform. The carriages on the far side were standing in the bay platform, which was normally used by trains from the Carmarthen Branch. The sidings to the north of the station can be seen in the distance in this scene recorded on 18th March 1961. (R.Patterson)

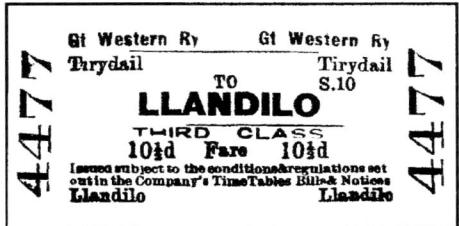

5.   Looking south from the up platform, 2-6-4T no. 42395 was seen arriving with an early morning train from Swansea, whilst the overnight "York Mail" waits in the down platform before continuing its journey to Swansea on 18th March 1961. (E.Wilmshurst)

6.   This elevated view shows BR 2-6-4T no.80069 departing from the down platform with a train for Swansea. The bay platform road and adjacent siding were noticeably empty when this scene was recorded in 1962. (D.Johnson/R.S.Carpenter coll.)

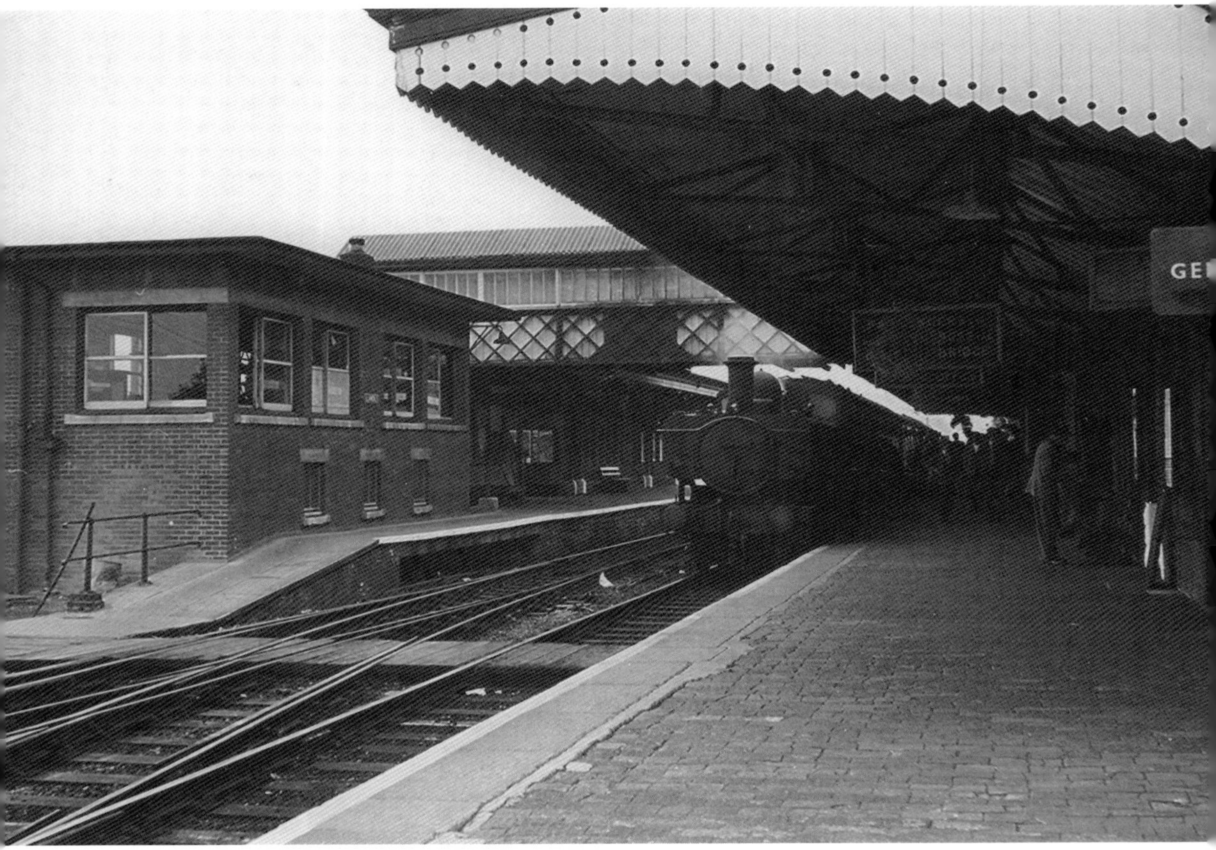

7. The austere signal box constructed in 1955 is conspicuous in this view whilst former GWR 0-6-0PT no.7444 stands in the up platform at the head of a train it has hauled from Carmarthen. This photograph was recorded on 2nd August 1963, a month before the Carmarthen Branch was closed. (E.Wilmshurst)

Other photographs appear in the companion album *Craven Arms to Llandeilo*.

Gt. Western Ry. Gt. Western Ry
BYNEA BYNEA
929 929
TO
AMMANFORD
Via Pantyffynnon
10d THIRD CLASS 10d
Issued subject to the conditions & regulations set out in the Company's Time Tables, Bills & Notices
Ammanford Ammanford

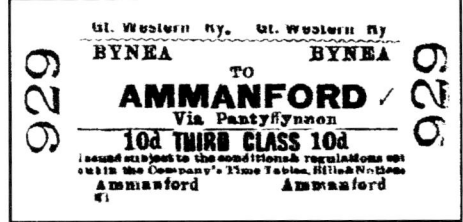

8.   The scene at this once proud station now presents a very different picture. All that remains are the two platforms, adorned with basic shelters for passenger comfort. Although the passing loop is still in place, it is rarely used and the up platform normally caters for both up and down trains. The two levels of platform height are a legacy of the construction of the station by the Vale of Towy Railway in 1858. This view of the station in its current guise, looking south, was recorded on 27th September 2008. (J.F.Organ)

9.   A view in the opposite direction on the same occasion shows the all too familiar scene of minimal care of track and provision of passenger comfort. (J.F.Organ)

FFAIRFACH

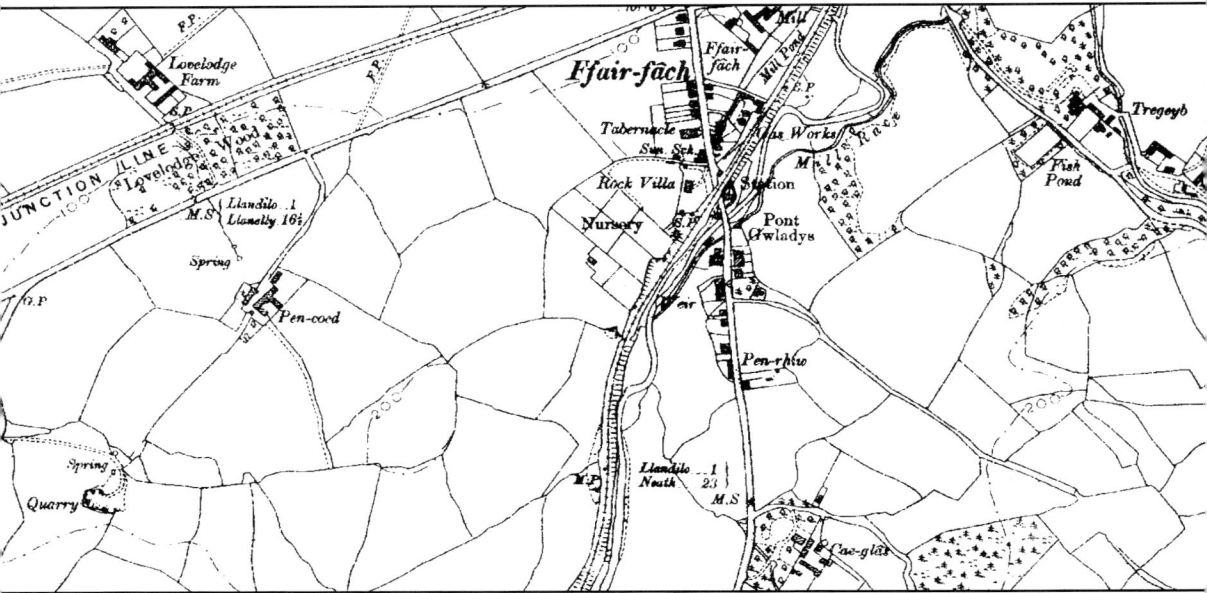

III.　　Ffairfach is one mile from Llandeilo. The two settlements are separated by the River Towy, which is also crossed by an impressive stone built road bridge dating from 1848. This survey from 1907 shows the full extent of the small station as originally constructed. Staffing ceased in May 1961 and term "Halt" was dropped in May 1969.

10.　　This view of the station was recorded on 16th June 1963 when the station buildings, signal box and goods siding where still in place. Just the former down platform and a shelter now suffice. There was a gasworks siding in 1866-1961. (R.Patterson)

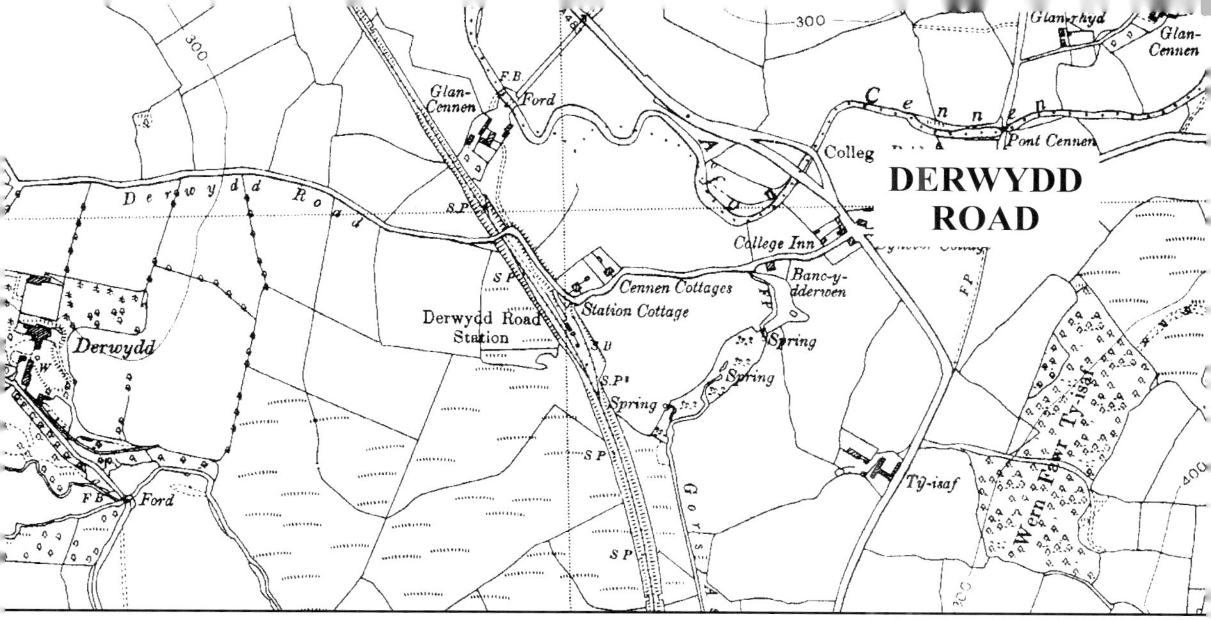

DERWYDD ROAD

IV. The summit of the route between Llandeilo and Swansea is reached here, which at 229ft is the third highest point on the Central Wales Line. The 1948 survey shows the station complete with a small goods yard, which closed on 14th March 1966, as did the signal box and loop.

11. The station, retained a typical GWR signal box when this view towards Llandeilo was recorded on 16th June 1963. Passenger service ceased on 3rd May 1954. (R.Patterson)

12. No sign of the station remained when this scene was photographed of Class 5MT 4-6-0 no.44767 hauling a southbound special excursion over the summit at Derwydd on 23rd May 1993. About ¾ mile to the south was Limestone Branch, from about 1876 to 1969. (D.Trevor Rowe)

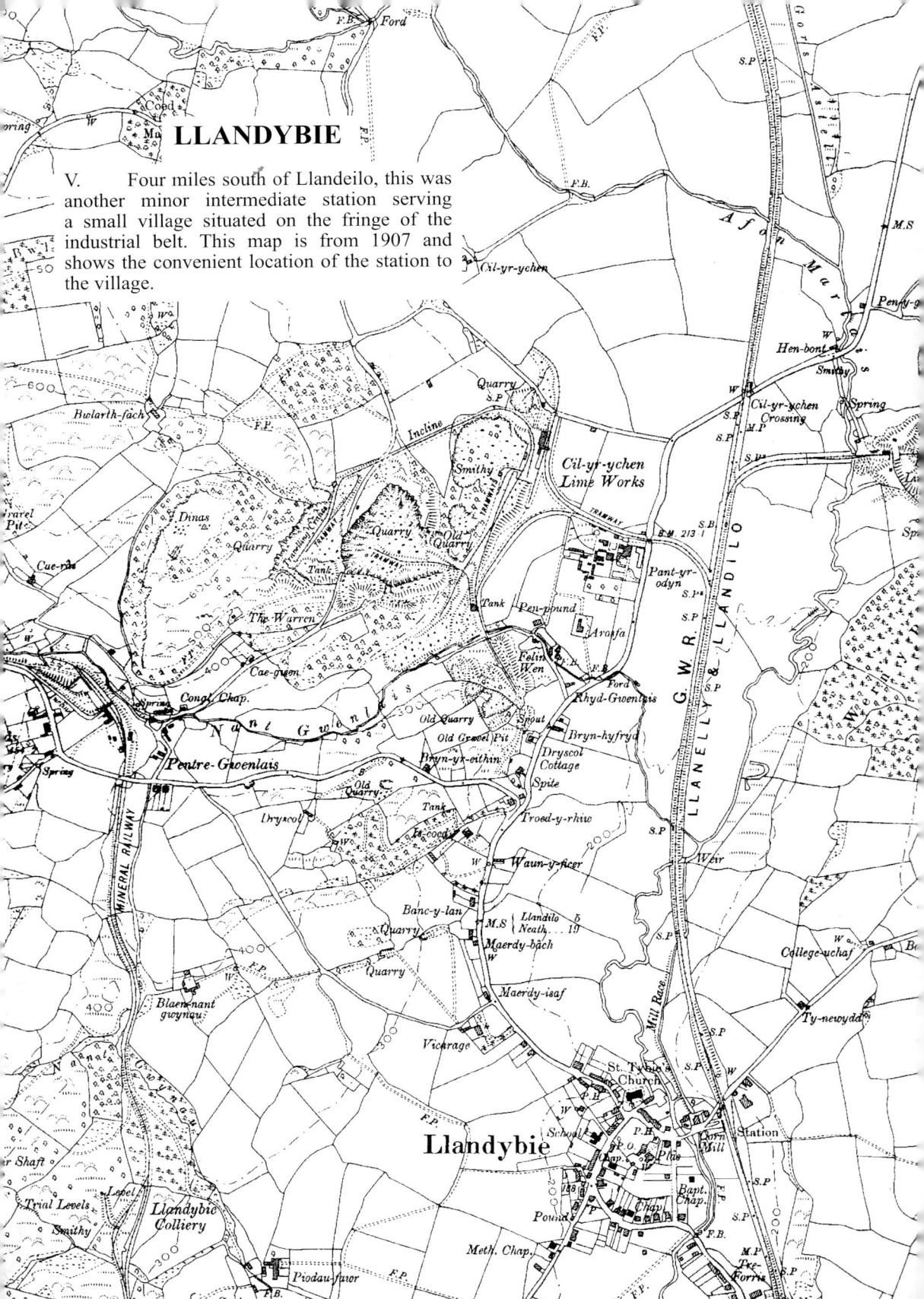

LLANDYBIE

V.   Four miles south of Llandeilo, this was another minor intermediate station serving a small village situated on the fringe of the industrial belt. This map is from 1907 and shows the convenient location of the station to the village.

13.   This view looking north, which shows the signal box and level crossing gates still in position, was recorded on 26th December 1981. All that now remains is the platform and a basic shelter. Goods traffic had ceased on 3rd May 1965 and the loop closed. (F.A.Blencowe)

14.   Although photographed on the same occasion, the signal box still retained the former name of Llandebie unlike the station, which had been renamed in 1971 with the Welsh interpretation of the name. The box closed in July 1985. (F.A.Blencowe)

AMMANFORD & TIRYDAIL

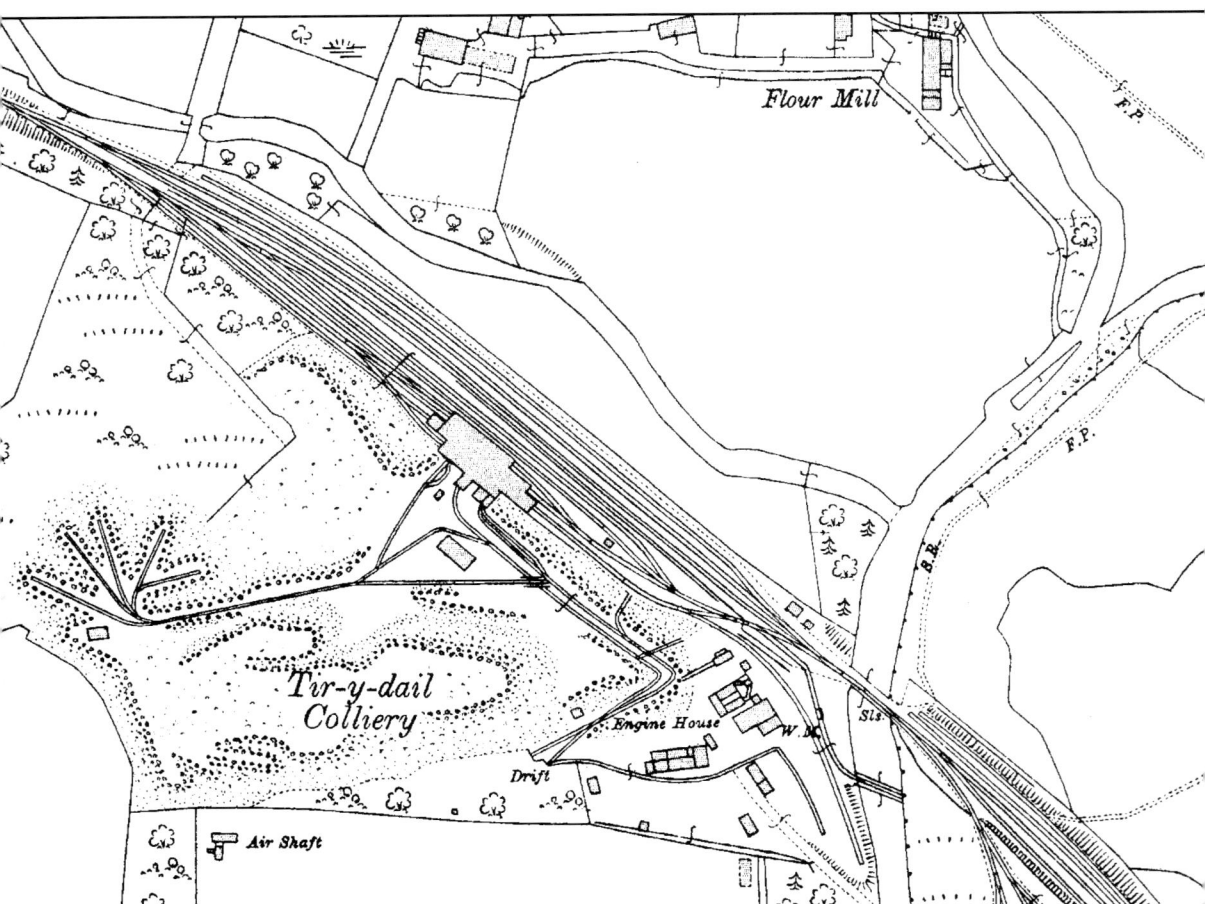

VI.   The Llanelly Railway & Dock Company opened a station here in 1841. Originally named Duffryn, it was renamed Tirydail by the GWR in 1889 whilst Ammanford Station was situated on the nearby Brynamman Branch. Following   closure of the latter station in 1958, Tirydail was renamed Ammanford & Tirydail in 1960 whilst Tirydail has been dropped from the name during the last decade. The 1916 survey shows the extensive sidings to the north of the station which served Tirydail Colliery, whilst the steeply graded GWR branch to Tumble continued beyond the sidings. The signal box was in use from 1897 to 1985.

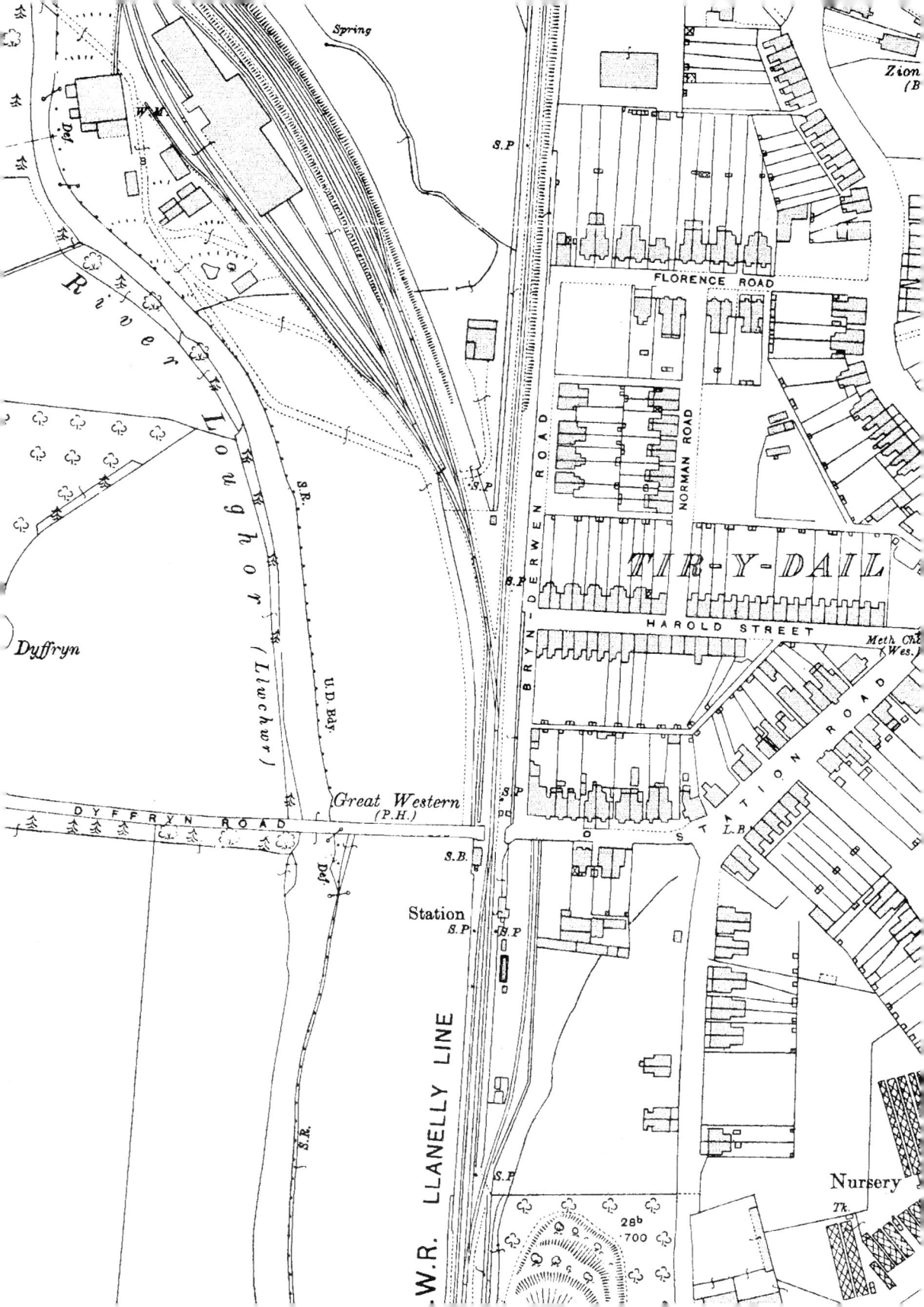

Spring

Zion
(B

Def.

W M

S.P

FLORENCE ROAD

River Loughor (Llwchwr)

S.R.

NORMAN ROAD

BRYN-DERWEN ROAD

S.P

TIR-Y-DAIL

Dyffryn

U.D. Bdy.

HAROLD STREET

Meth. Ch
Wes.

STATION ROAD

Great Western
(P.H.)

S.P

DYFFRYN ROAD

L.B.

Def.

S.B.

Station
S.P
S.P

Nursery

Tk

G.W.R. LLANELLY LINE

S.P

28ᵇ
700

S.P

15.   We are now entering the western extremities of the South Wales coal mining area, whilst other industrial remains such as limestone quarrying are also in evidence. Our first view, looking north, shows a typically GWR complex with a fine array of lower quadrant signals. This scene was recorded on 28th September 1960. Half a mile to the south was Parcyrhun Halt from 1936 to 1955. (H.C.Casserley)

16.   The up "York Mail" hauled by class 5MT 4-6-0 no.73095 was recorded as it passed through the station en route from Swansea to York on 5th June 1963. This service was destined to cease one year later, following the closure of Swansea Victoria. The goods yard closed on 2nd November 1964 and the loop lasted until March 1965. (R.Priestley/R.S.Carpenter coll.)

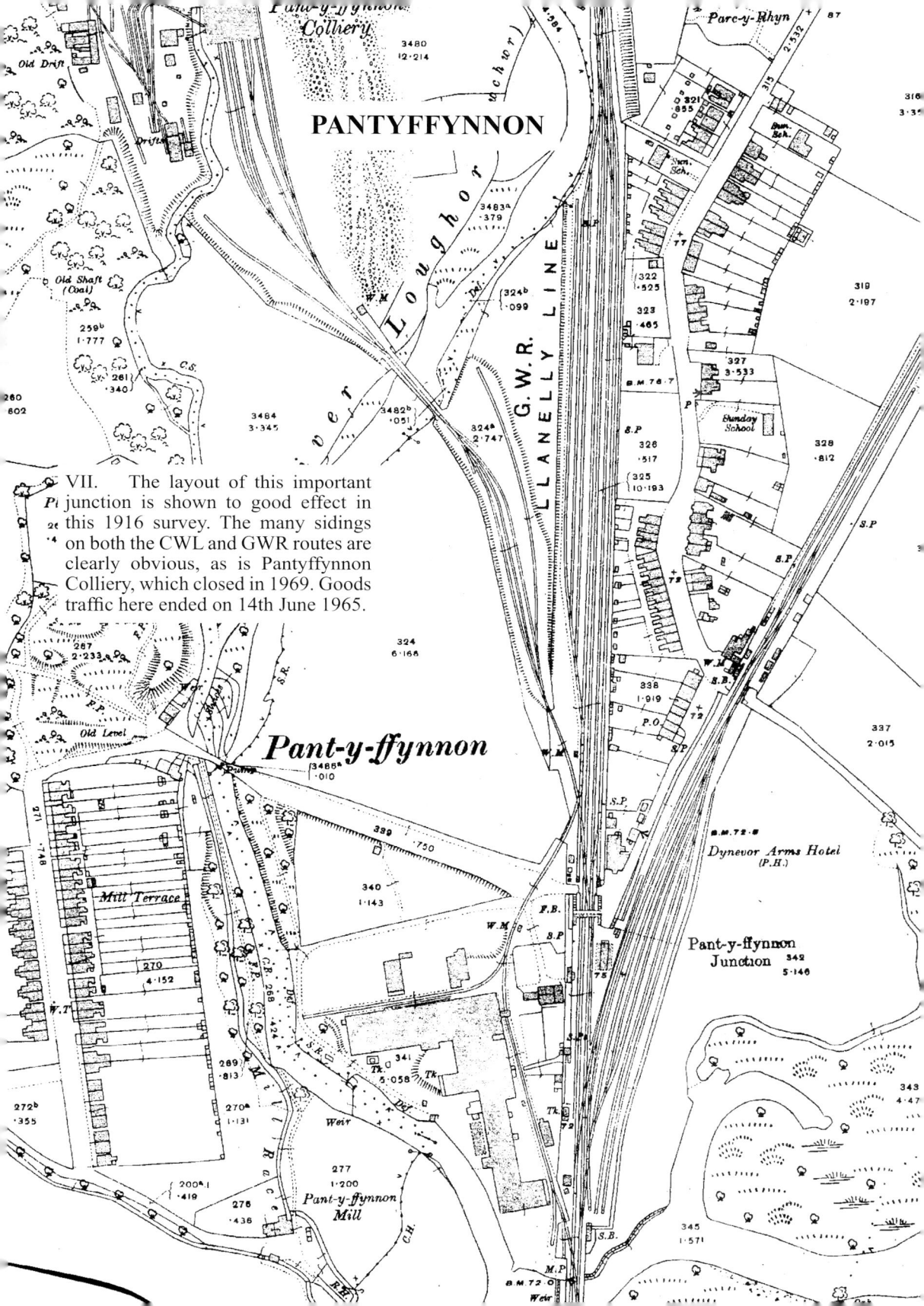

PANTYFFYNNON

VII. The layout of this important junction is shown to good effect in this 1916 survey. The many sidings on both the CWL and GWR routes are clearly obvious, as is Pantyffynnon Colliery, which closed in 1969. Goods traffic here ended on 14th June 1965.

Pant-y-ffynnon

Pant-y-ffynnon Junction

Dynevor Arms Hotel (P.H.)

Mill Terrace

Pant-y-ffynnon Mill

17.   The Central Wales section of the station is shown in this view looking north, with the characteristic GWR buildings and footbridge. The platform serving the Brynamman branch is to the right of the photograph, with the multitude of sidings beyond, in this scene recorded on 8th September 1951. (H.C.Casserley)

18.   Both platforms are seen from across the tracks of the Brynamman line on the same occasion. A fine array of GWR lower quadrant signals are very conspicuous in this scene, whilst a large number of fire buckets were hanging on the side of the station building. (H.C.Casserley)

19.   0-6-0PT no.3719 was photographed as it arrived at the up platform whilst hauling a local train from Pontardulais to Llandilo. Former GWR locomotives of this type were invariably used on local passenger services, such as this example pictured on 29th April 1961. (R.M.Casserley)

20.   Following the withdrawal of the illustrious Fowler 2-6-4Ts, the later BR Standard Class variation replaced them during the final period of steam haulage on the Central Wales Line. 2-6-4T no.80069 was viewed as it departed from the down platform with a Craven Arms to Swansea train on 15th June 1963. (R.Patterson)

21.   DMU no.C610 was recorded as it approached the down platform with a southbound train heading for Swansea via Llanelli. The level crossing was protected by gates until November 1983. The photograph is from 19th September 1979. (T.Heavyside)

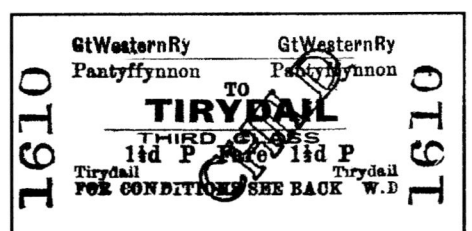

Gt Western Ry   Gt Western Ry
Pantyffynnon   Pantyffynnon
TO
TIRYDAIL
THIRD CLASS
1¼d P   Fare   1¼d P
Tirydail   Tirydail
FOR CONDITIONS SEE BACK   W.D
1610   1610

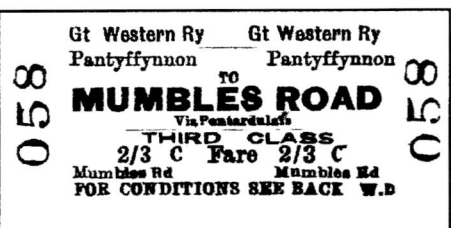

Gt Western Ry   Gt Western Ry
Pantyffynnon   Pantyffynnon
TO
MUMBLES ROAD
Via Pontardulais
THIRD CLASS
2/3 C   Fare   2/3 C
Mumbles Rd   Mumbles Rd
FOR CONDITIONS SEE BACK   W.D
058   050

22.   Unlike many of the stations on the route, the principal buildings remained at this location. They housed a train crew depot for local colliery and open cast workings for many years. Pantyffynnon South Signal Box in the distance is now the only one remaining in working order on the Central Wales Line. This controls the entire 79 mile route between Craven Arms and Pantyffynnon by token and telephone, the remaining section to Llanelli being under the control of the signalling centre at Port Talbot. Only the down line remained in use when this scene was recorded on 16th September 1990. (M.J.Stretton)

23.   The rusty rails of the closed GWR branch and sidings were disappearing under grass and weeds, whilst the remaining track of our route appears to be well maintained. However on a more positive note, the disused up platform had been planted with attractive plants and shrubs when this view of the station was taken on 27th September 2008. (J.F.Organ)

SOUTH OF PANTYFFYNNON

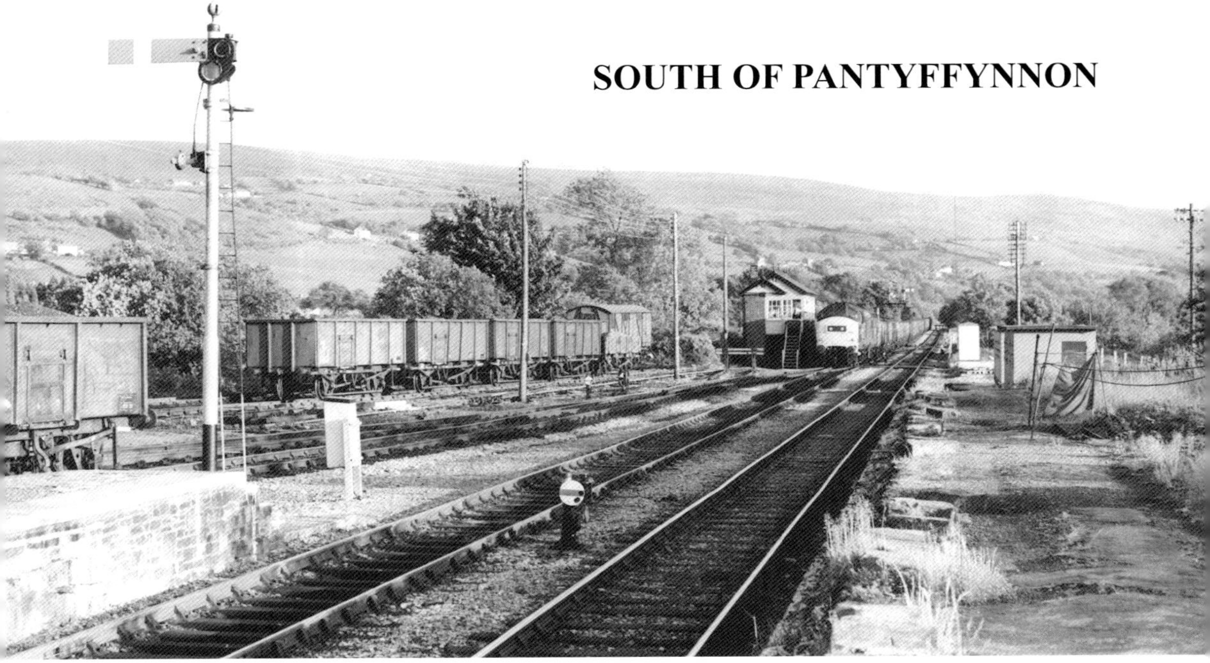

24. A freight train, hauled by no.37 279, was viewed passing the South Signal Box on 14th June 1983, whilst the mountains of the western fringe of the industrial valleys of South Wales dominate the skyline. This part of the route was singled on 31st December 1967. (T.Heavyside)

25. No. 37 279 was photographed as it entered the yard whilst hauling a long train of empty coal trucks from the south. These would ultimately be hauled to the various collieries at the head of the Brynamman branch. This impressive scene was witnessed shortly after illustration no.24 was recorded. (T.Heavyside)

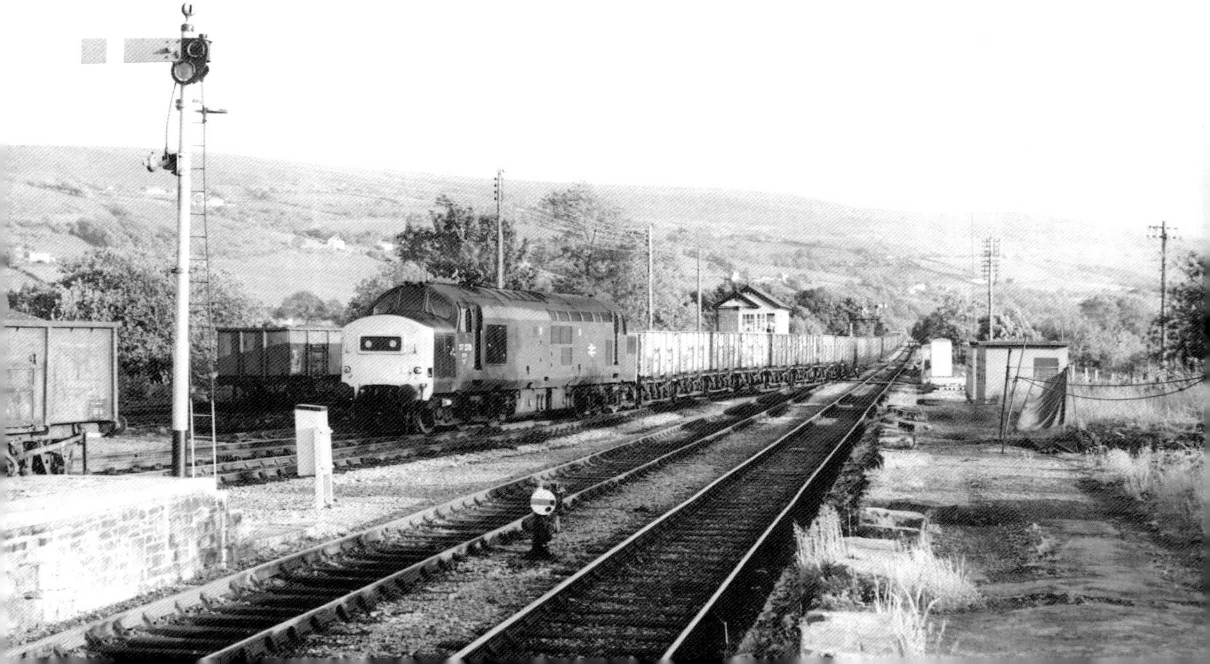

26.   An engineering train hauled by no.37 304 leaves the branch line and heads south towards Pontarddulais. The former CWL up line was only in use at that time in order to provide access to the coal washeries at Pantyffynnon and Wernos, located north of the station, when this view was recorded on 1st September 1985. (P.Jones)

27.   Nos 37 208 and 37 234 were viewed as they paused near the signal box, prior to running up the branch to collect a loaded coal train from one of the colliery disposal points also recorded on 1st September 1985. The branch lines to Brynamman and Gwaun-cae-Gurwen will be covered in a future Middleton Press publication. (P.Jones)

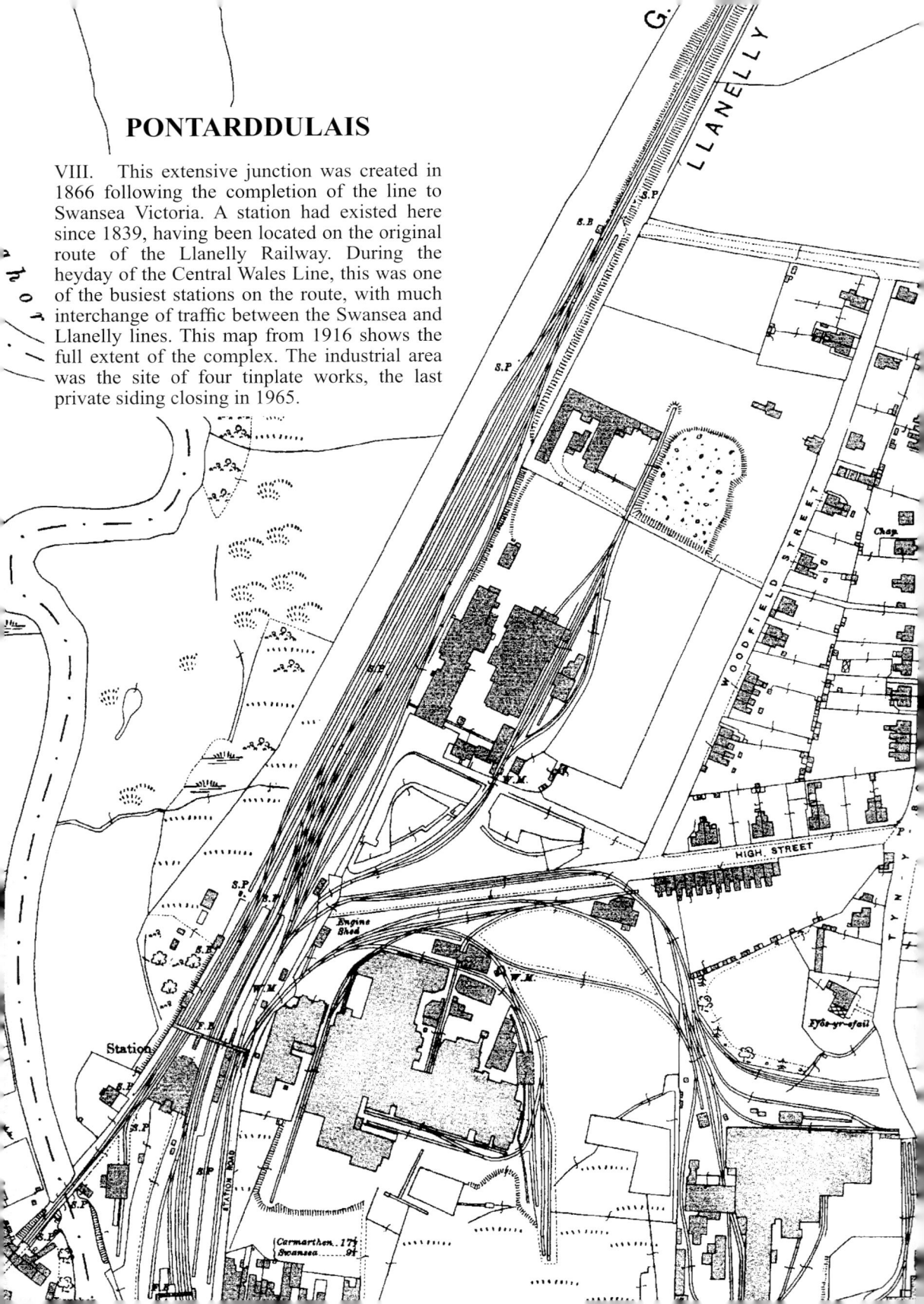

PONTARDDULAIS

VIII. This extensive junction was created in 1866 following the completion of the line to Swansea Victoria. A station had existed here since 1839, having been located on the original route of the Llanelly Railway. During the heyday of the Central Wales Line, this was one of the busiest stations on the route, with much interchange of traffic between the Swansea and Llanelly lines. This map from 1916 shows the full extent of the complex. The industrial area was the site of four tinplate works, the last private siding closing in 1965.

28.   The long footbridge which extended across the entire width of the station is shown to good advantage in this view looking south. The photograph was taken from the down platform of the Swansea line on 8th September 1951. (H.C.Casserley)

29.   On the same occasion the platforms of the Llanelly line were recorded. The commencement of the single line section can be seen in the distance, just before the line enters the short tunnel; only 88yds in length. (H.C.Casserley)

30.   The signalman from Pontardulais Junction Station Signal Box is about to hand over the token to the driver of 0-6-0PT no.5702, which is arriving with a train bound for Llanelly on 26th May 1956. The box closed on 30th December 1967. (N.L Browne/M.J.Stretton coll.)

31   Former Burry Port & Gwendraeth Valley Railway 0-6-0T no.2198 was viewed whilst on shunting duty in the sidings to the east of the station. Note the shovel wedged behind the handrail in front of the chimney in this delightful scene from 26th May 1956. (N.L.Browne/M.J.Stretton coll.)

32.   The wide central platform was a great asset in view of the large amount of passenger and freight transfers between the two lines. This picture is from 11th July 1958. (R.M.Casserley)

33.   For many years the local passenger trains on both routes were hauled by the ubiquitous GWR pannier tank locomotives. With clear instructions on the station name board for passengers intending to continue their journey to the north, no.7776 was photographed as it arrived with a train from Llanelly on 1st August 1958. (G.Adams/M.J.Stretton coll.)

34.   On the same occasion no.1614, one of the smaller type of 0-6-0PTs built in 1949, was recorded as it passed the down platform of the Swansea line whilst engaged in shunting operations. (G.Adams/M.J.Stretton coll.)

35.   Viewed from the footbridge, the extensive sidings to the north of the station were very conspicuous in this scene recorded on 28th September 1960. By 1967, their number was down to three. (H.C.Casserley)

36.   Various features betray the GWR origin of this section of the Central Wales route. This is another view to the north on the same occasion. (H.C.Casserley)

37.   0-6-0PT no.8749 was replenishing its water tanks when it was photographed at the south end of the Swansea line down platform on 28th September 1960. The road over the level crossing in the distance climbed steeply in order to cross the Llanelly line above the tunnel seen in other views. (H.C.Casserley)

38. No. 3719 had just arrived with a train from Llanelly when it was pictured alongside the fine GWR signal box on 21st August 1961. (E.Wilmshurst)

39. Long term resident of Swansea Paxton Street Depot, 2-6-4T no. 42394 was seen as it arrived at the down platform with a Shrewsbury to Swansea train in 1962. (D.Johnson/R.S.Carpenter coll.)

40. Amazingly all that now remains of this once impressive junction station is the former down platform of the Llanelli line, adorned with a basic shelter for "passenger comfort". Note the enormous amount of tree and undergrowth that now occupies the former site of the station infrastructure in this scene recorded on 27th September 2008. (J.F.Organ)

41. Single car unit no.153 323 was photographed as it arrived at the now very basic station with a Shrewsbury to Swansea, via Llanelli, service on the same occasion. The goods yard closed on 7th June 1965. (J.F.Organ)

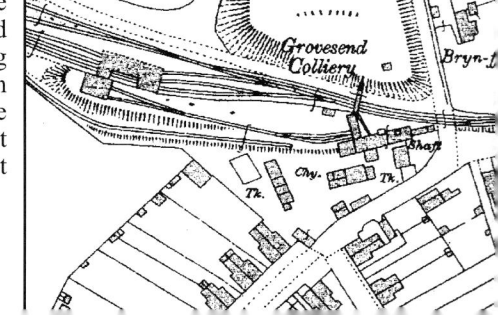

1X.   A 1916 survey at 20 ins to 1 mile scale shows the connection diverging from the Swansea line, which served the Bryn Lliw and Grovesend Colliery complex. Following the closure of the main line in June 1964, this section remained in operation for a further 10 years to provide access to the collieries. This was abandoned after a direct connection from the colliery to the nearby Swansea District Line was constructed in 1974.

SOUTH OF PONTARDDULAIS

←   42. One of the familiar NCB 0-6-0STs was recorded as it was engaged in shunting operations in the exchange sidings at Pontarddulais on 24th May 1973, during the final decade of coal production at Grovesend. (T.Heavyside)

←   43. Wreathed in steam, Peckett 0-6-0ST no. 1426 was photographed as it departed from the loading gantries at Brynlliw Colliery in May 1973. This locomotive now resides in Swansea Industrial and Maritime Museum. (T.Heavyside)

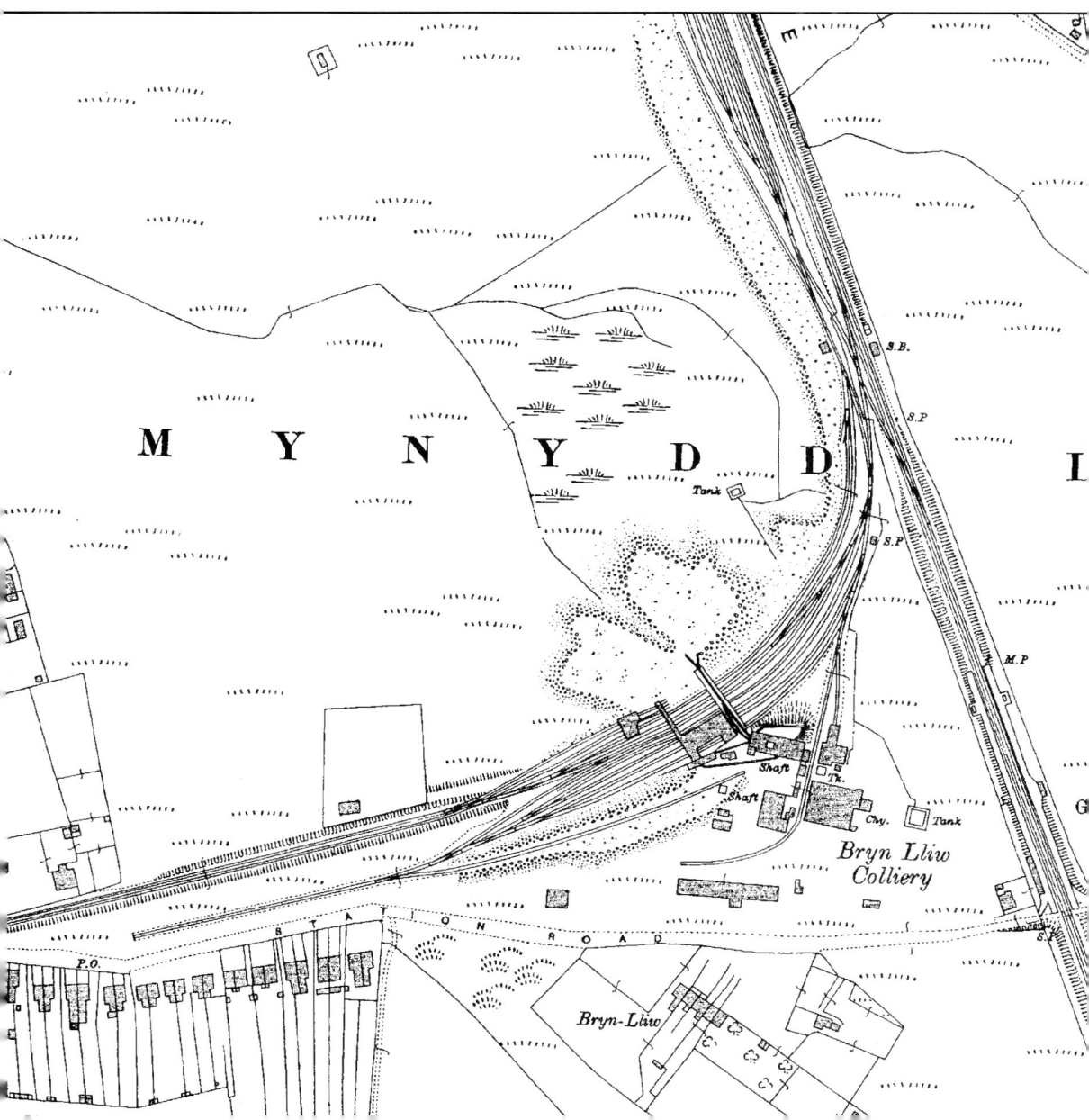

44. No.1426 is seen at work in the exchange sidings at Grovesend on 20th September 1979, shortly before it was withdrawn from service. Public platforms were in use from 1st January 1910 until 6th June 1932. (T.Heavyside)

45. Nos 37 236 and 37 294 were photographed as they hauled a heavy load of coal wagons over the new connection onto the Swansea District Line on 6th November 1981. The train is leaving a loop beyond the junction. This connection was to be short lived, the colliery closing in 1985. The remaining stocks of coal were cleared by October 1989. (M.Hughes)

GORSEINON

46.   Framed by a characteristic LNWR style footbridge, 0-6-0PT no.7776 arrives at the station with a local train from Swansea on 6th August 1958. Note the upper quadrant signal mounted at a high level, a common feature on lines inherited by British Railways from the LMS. (G.Adams/M.J.Stretton coll.)

47.   This view towards Swansea shows the typical LNWR architecture and infrastructure in this scene from 16th June 1963. A year later the line was closed and all is now lost without trace at this location under a new bypass scheme. (R.Patterson)

Mountain Colliery

Melin Mon...
(Disused)

W.M.

Laundry

MINERAL RAILWAY

CECIL

Chy.

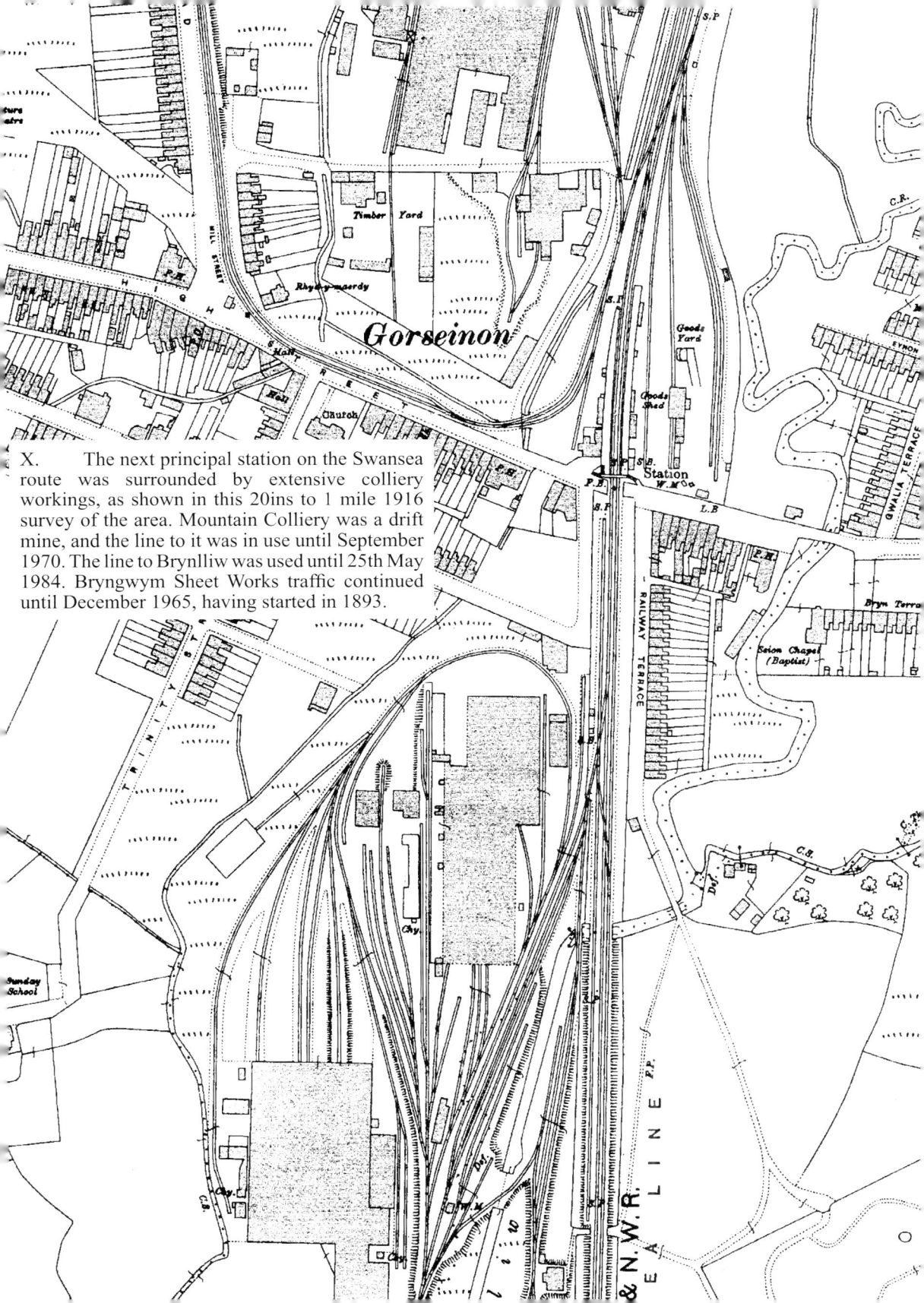

Gorseinon

X.　　　The next principal station on the Swansea route was surrounded by extensive colliery workings, as shown in this 20ins to 1 mile 1916 survey of the area. Mountain Colliery was a drift mine, and the line to it was in use until September 1970. The line to Brynlliw was used until 25th May 1984. Bryngwym Sheet Works traffic continued until December 1965, having started in 1893.

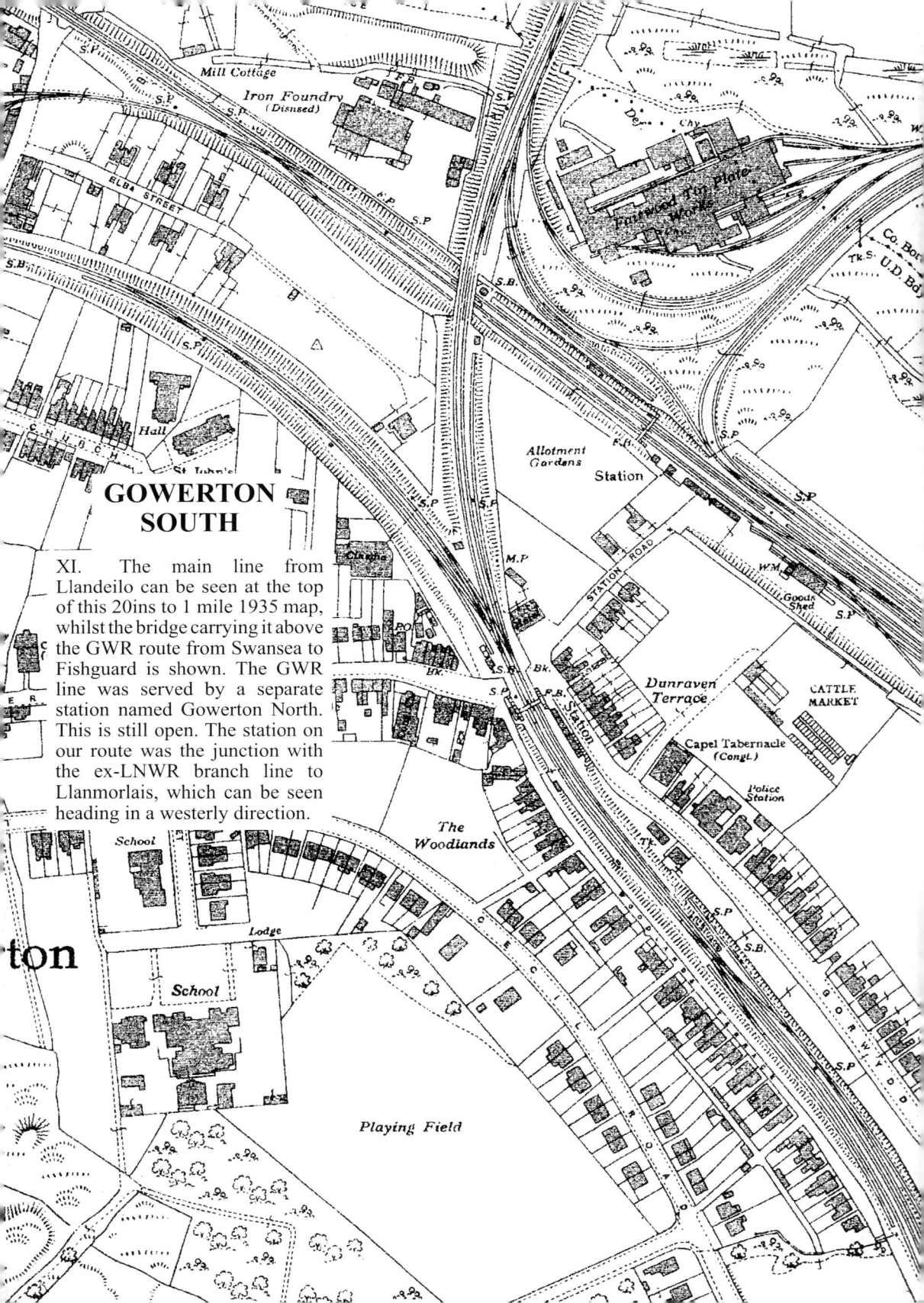

GOWERTON SOUTH

XI. The main line from Llandeilo can be seen at the top of this 20ins to 1 mile 1935 map, whilst the bridge carrying it above the GWR route from Swansea to Fishguard is shown. The GWR line was served by a separate station named Gowerton North. This is still open. The station on our route was the junction with the ex-LNWR branch line to Llanmorlais, which can be seen heading in a westerly direction.

Mill Cottage

Iron Foundry
(Disused)

ELBA STREET

Hall

St John's

Fairwood Tin Plate Works

CATTLE MARKET

Allotment Gardens

Station

STATION ROAD

Goods Shed

Dunraven Terrace

Capel Tabernacle
(Congl.)

Police Station

The Woodlands

School

Lodge

School

Playing Field

48. This view of the station in 1912 shows the line from Llandeilo entering from the right. The line diverging to the left beyond the footbridge was the five mile long Llanmorlais branch, which lost its passenger traffic in January 1931, although freight traffic associated with the Elba Steel Works and Cefn Goleu Colliery continued until the closure of the Swansea line. (Lens of Sutton coll.)

49. A view from the same era, looking south, shows the sraff of one shift. The suffix SOUTH was added in January 1950. (Lens of Sutton coll.)

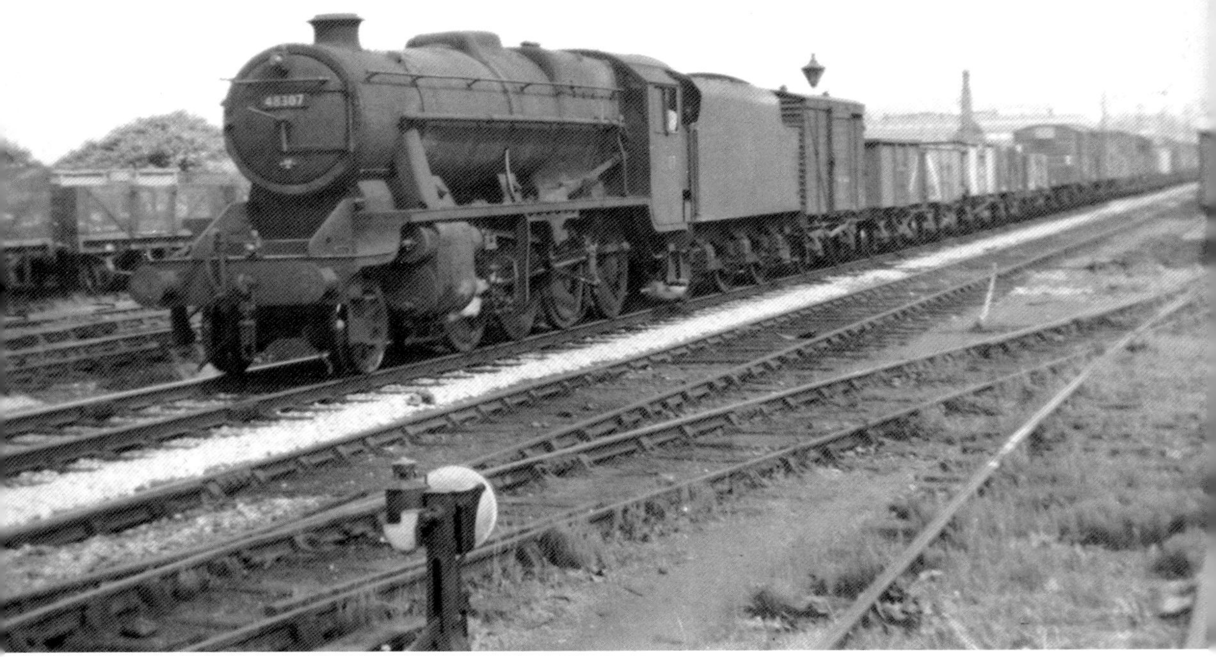

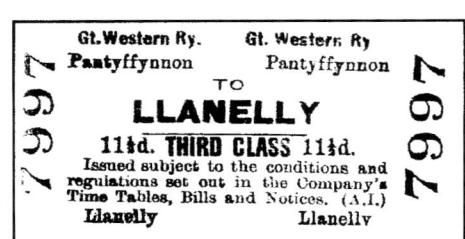

50. The mainstay of freight haulage on the Central Wales Line was for many years the incomparable class 8F 2-8-0s. No.48307 was recorded as it departed from Gowerton with a heavy mixed freight in 1958. (D.K.Jones coll)

7997 Gt.Western Ry. Pantyffynnon Gt. Western Ry Pantyffynnon 7997

TO

LLANELLY

11½d. THIRD CLASS 11½d.

Issued subject to the conditions and regulations set out in the Company's Time Tables, Bills and Notices. (A.I.)

Llanelly Llanelly

Gt.Western Ry. LLANDILO Gt.Western Ry. LLANDILO

TO

PONTARDULAIS

1/1 PARLY,(3rd.Cls) 1/1

Issued subject to the conditions & regulations set out in the Company's Time Tables Books and Bills. (C.G.)

Pontardulais Pontardulais 1536

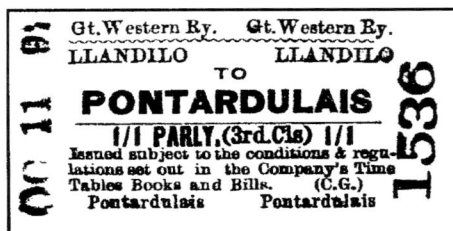

51.   Stanier 4-6-0 no.45145 was simmering gently in the winter sunshine when it was photographed prior to departure from the down platform with a Swansea bound train in February 1960. The signal box here and at Glassbrooks Colliery closed on 14th June 1964. (D.K.Jones coll.)

52.   Class 5MT 4-6-0 no.73036 was viewed as it approached the station from the north whilst hauling a Shrewsbury to Swansea service during August 1961. The goods yard was in use until the line closed. (D.K.Jones coll.)

XII.   Despite its close proximity to the industrial regions of the area, the next stations on the route were set in attractive locations. The small colliery to the east was still extant at the time of this 1916 survey, but was destined to close prior to World War II.

Chy.

Chy.

S.P.

Quarry

E.S.P.

W.M.

Quarry

Union Bdy.
Def.

Slant

Slant

Qua

Dunv
C

Quarry

S.B.

Engine House

Burial Ground

Indt. Chap.
(Welsh)

W.T.

Quarry

Old Slant

W.T.

T.S.

O.S.

S.P.

Station

P.O.

W.T.

S.P.

w   a   n   t

DUNVANT

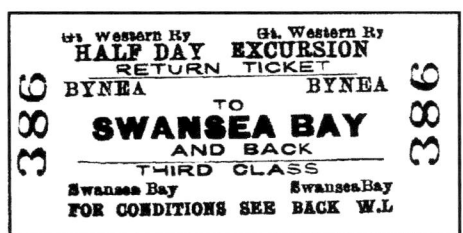
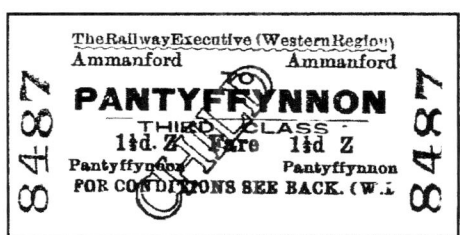

53.   The station, with its characteristic high gabled roof, was viewed looking towards Swansea on 16th June 1963. Goods service lasted to the end. (R.Patterson)

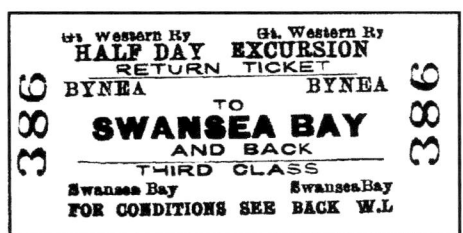

Gt. Western Ry   Gt. Western Ry
HALF DAY EXCURSION
RETURN TICKET
BYNEA   BYNEA
TO
SWANSEA BAY
AND BACK
THIRD CLASS
Swansea Bay   Swansea Bay
FOR CONDITIONS SEE BACK W.L

386   386

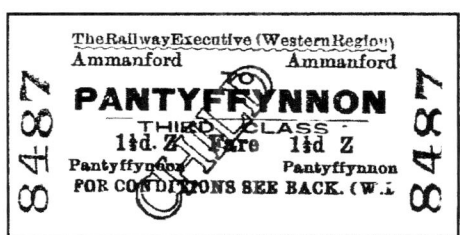

The Railway Executive (Western Region)
Ammanford   Ammanford
PANTYFFYNNON
THIRD CLASS
1½d. Z   Fare   1½d. Z
Pantyffynnon   Pantyffynnon
FOR CONDITIONS SEE BACK. (W.I

8487   8487

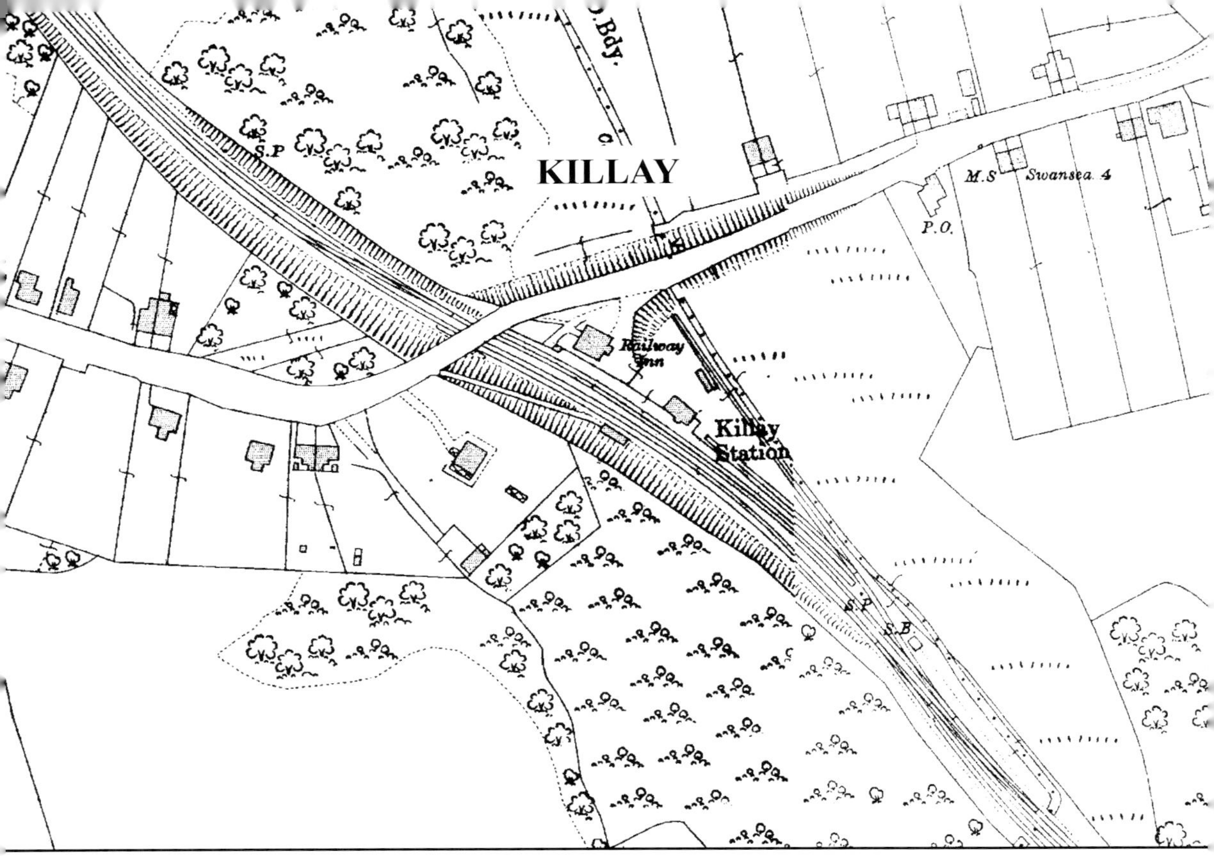

KILLAY

XIII.   Also located in a delightful woodland setting, this station served a small community, as shown on this map of 1919. Only the Railway Inn and some isolated farms were in the vicinity. The Clyne Tramway diverged east of the station, served a brickworks and a colliery and joined the Swansea & Mumbles Railway near Mumbles Road.

54.   Less than five miles from Swansea, the attractive station situated in Cline Woods was recorded on 16th June 1963, whilst a rake of coal wagons occupied the goods siding. The yard was in use until June 1964, when the line closed completely. (R.Patterson)

MUMBLES ROAD

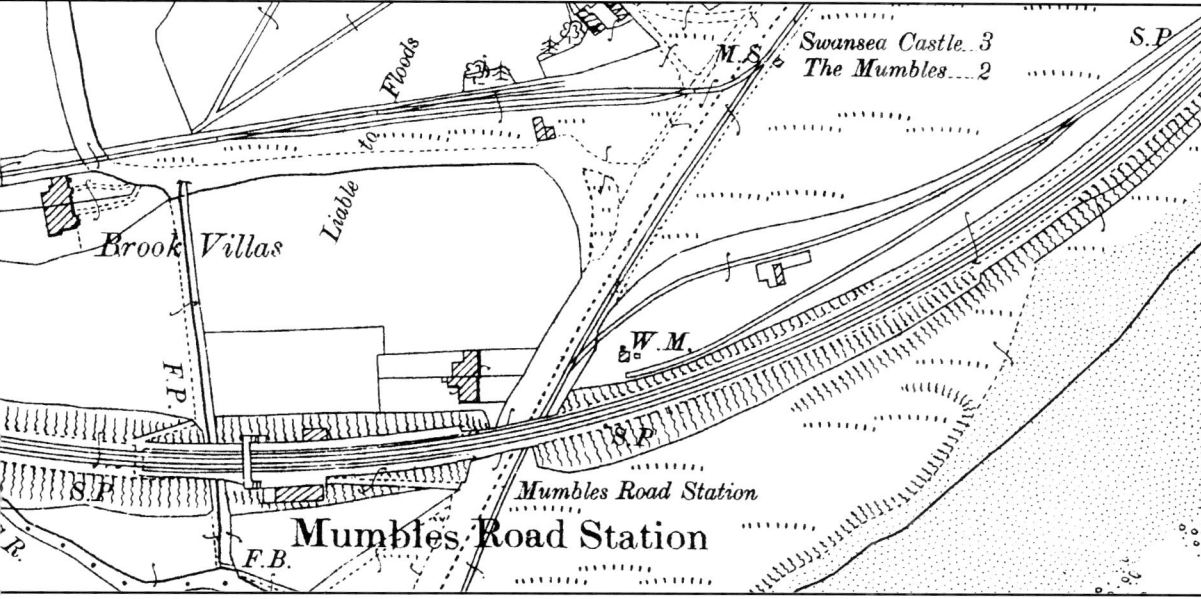

XIV.   The coastal section of the route is from the 1899 edition. The adjacent Swansea & Mumbles
Railway had a connection with our route until July 1952.

55.   The line joined the coast for the final part of the journey to Swansea. This view of the station
at Mumbles Road, looking west, was recorded prior to the grouping of 1923.
(Lens of Sutton coll.)

56.　　A later easterly view of the station features another characteristic LNWR style footbridge, whilst the early style lamp standards have been retained. This is the scene on 18th August 1962. (R.Patterson)

57.　　A former GWR 0-6-0PT was photographed as it arrived at the station with a train from Swansea to Llandilo in 1962. Freight traffic here continued to the end of passenger operation. (D.Johnson/R.S.Carpenter coll.)

EAST OF
MUMBLES ROAD

58.   No.8414, one of the later Hawksworth designed 0-6-0PTs, runs along the coast near St.Helens, hauling a train bound for Pontardulais on a sunny Summer evening in 1960. (P.Jones)

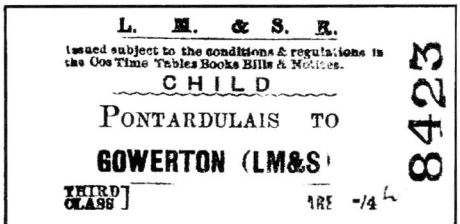

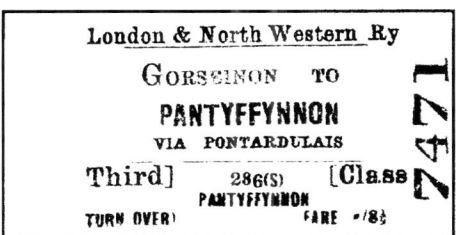

SWANSEA BAY

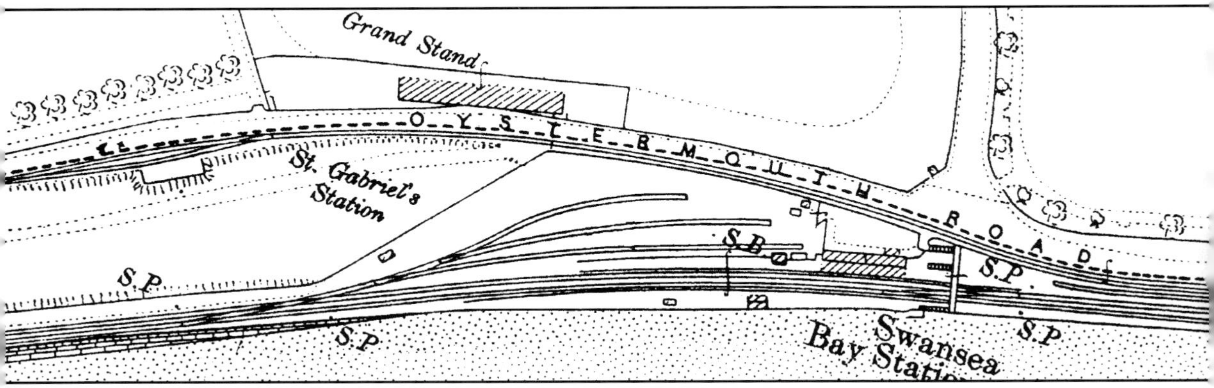

XV. 1899 edition.

May 1948

SHREWSBURY, CRAVEN ARMS, BUILTH ROAD, CARMARTHEN, and SWANSEA

Miles from Shrewsbury	Week Days only	p.m	am	a.m	a.m	a.m		p.m	p.m	p.m	p.m	p.m	p.m	a.m	p.m	p.m	a.m	p.m	p.m	p.m	p.m	p.m.
50	London (Euston) .dep	10 50	..	..	..	..	..	..	..	..	..	..	..	..	..	..	8 30	..	..	..	..	12B5
	" (Paddington) "	..	..	..	..	12Z5	..	..	..	..	..	..	..	..	..	..	9 10	..	..	..	..	11 10
50	Birmingham (N St) "	11 5	..	..	..	..	..	..	..	..	..	..	..	8F25	..	..	11 0	..	..	..	..	1 50
	" (Snow Hill) "	a.m	..	..	..	4 10	..	..	..	..	..	..	..	8 36	..	..	11 56	..	..	..	..	3 0
86	Manchester (L Rd) "	12 30	..	..	..	..	..	..	..	..	..	..	..	9J10	..	..	12 15	..	..	..	..	3 0
86	Liverpool (L. St.) "	12 5	..	..	..	..	..	..	..	..	..	..	..	9 25	..	..	11 40	..	..	..	..	2 50
86	Birkenhead A ...	10K5	..	..	..	..	..	..	..	..	..	..	..	8B30	..	..	10h35	..	..	..	..	2B35
86	Crewe .... "	2 15	..	..	..	..	..	..	..	..	..	..	..	10 45	..	..	1 20	..	..	..	..	4 9
		a.m (FC York to Swansea (Victoria) (Tables 146 and 86))	am	a.m	a.m	a.m		p.m	p.m	p.m	p.m	p.m	p.m	p.m	p.m	p.m	p.m	p.m	p.m	p.m	p.m	p.m
	Shrewsbury ....dep	3 45	..	..	..	6 25	..	..	..	..	..	..	..	12T30	..	..	2T40	..	..	..	..	5T30
12¾	Church Stretton .... "	..	..	..	..	7 0	..	..	..	..	..	..	..	12 55	..	..	..	..	..	..	..	5 55
19½	Craven Arms and Stokesay arr	4 17	..	..	..	7 17	..	..	..	..	..	..	..	1 8	..	..	3 13	..	..	..	..	6 6
	Craven Arms and Stokesay dep	4 22	..	..	..	7 40	..	..	..	..	..	..	..	1 15	..	2 20	3 20	..	..	..	..	6 10
22½	Broome	..	..	..	..	7 46	..	..	..	..	..	..	..	..	..	2 27	3 26	..	..	..	..	..
24¾	Hopton Heath	..	..	..	..	7 51	..	..	..	..	..	..	..	..	..	2 33	3 31	..	..	..	..	6 21
27¾	Bucknell	4 36	..	..	..	7 57	..	..	..	..	..	..	..	1 31	..	2 40	3 37	..	..	..	..	6 27
32	Knighton	4 48	..	..	..	8 6	..	..	..	..	..	..	..	1 41	..	2 51	3 48	..	..	..	..	6 38
34½	Knucklas	..	..	..	..	8 13	..	..	..	..	..	..	..	..	..	2 56	..	..	..	..	..	..
38½	Llangunllo	..	..	..	..	8 25	..	..	..	..	..	..	..	1 58	..	3 8	..	..	..	..	..	6 54
41½	Llanbister Road C	..	..	..	..	8 31	..	..	..	..	..	..	..	2 4	..	3 14	..	..	..	..	..	6 59
45	Dolau	..	..	..	..	8 37	..	..	..	..	..	..	..	2 10	..	3 20	..	..	..	..	..	7 5
48	Penybont	..	..	..	..	8 44	..	..	..	..	..	..	..	2 17	..	3 28	4 16	..	..	..	..	7 12
51¾	Llandrindod Wells D ...	5 26	..	..	..	8 52	..	..	..	..	..	..	..	2 26	..	3 36	4 24	..	..	..	..	7 20
57½	Builth Road ....arr	5 37	..	..	..	9 3	..	..	..	..	..	..	..	2 37	..	3 47	4 35	..	..	..	..	7 31
84½	Brecon ....arr	..	..	..	..	1021	..	..	..	..	..	..	..	..	..	5 24	8 11	..	..	..	..	..
—	Builth Road ....dep	5 41	..	..		9 6	..	..	..	..	..		..	2 43		3 51	4 41	..		..	..	7 42
59¾	Cilmery Halt	..	..	..		9 11	..	..	..	..	..		..	..		3 57	..	..		..	..	..
62¼	Garth	..	..	..	W.R. Train	9 18	..	..	..	..	..	W.R. Train	..	2 51	W.R. Train	4 5	4 49	..	W.R. Train	..	..	7 53
64¼	Llangammarch Wells ..	5H55	..	..		9 23	..	..	..	..	..		..	2 56		4 11	4 54	..		..	..	7 59
67¾	Llanwrtyd Wells	6 2	..	..		9 33	..	..	..	..	..		..	3 3		4 18	5 1	..		..	..	8 7
74½	Cynghordy	..	..	..		9 47	..	..	..	..	..		..	3U17		4 34	..	..		..	..	..
79	Llandovery ...... arr	6 24	..	..		9 55	..	..	..	..	..		..	3 25		4 42	5 23	..		..	..	8 36
	Llandovery ...... dep	6 32	..	..	8 45	9 58	..	..	..	..	..	2 20	..	3 30	4 10	—	5 26	..	6 55	..	..	8 41
82¼	Llanwrda	6 38	..	..	8 54	10 4	..	..	..	..	..	2 28	..	3 36	4 18	Stop	5 32	..	7 3	..	..	8P47
84¼	Llangadock	6 44	..	..	9 0	10 9	..	..	..	..	..	2 33	..	3 40	4 23	..	5 36	..	7 9	..	..	8 51
86½	Glanrhyd Halt	..	..	..	9 4	..	..	..	..	..	..	2 37	..	..	4 27	..	..	..	7 13	..	..	..
88¼	Talley Road Halt	..	..	..	9 10	..	..	..	..	..	..	2 42	..	..	4 32	..	..	..	7 18	..	..	..
90¼	Llandilo ....arr	6 54	..	..	9 14	1019	..	..	..	..	..	2 46	..	3 50	4 36	..	5 46	..	7 22	..	..	9 1
—	Llandilo ....dep	8 0	..	..	..	1128	..	..	..	..	..	..	..	4 20	..	..	6 20	..	..	..	..	9 25
90½	Llandilo Bridge	8 4	..	..	..	1132	..	..	..	..	..	..	..	4 24	..	..	6 24	..	..	..	..	9 29
93	Golden Grove	8 10	..		..	1137	..	..		..	..	..	..	4 29	..	..	6 29	..	..	..		9 34
95½	Dryslwyn	8 15	..		..	1142	..	..		..	..	..	..	4 34	..	..	6 34	..	..	..		9 39
96¾	Llanarthney	8 20	..		..	1147	..	..		..	..	..	..	4 39	..	..	6 39	..	..	..		9 44
99½	Nantgaredig	8 26	..	W.R. Train	..	1153	..	..	W.R. Train	..	..	..	..	4 47	..	..	6 44	..	..	..		9 50
102¾	Abergwili	8 32	..		..	12 0	..	..		..	..	..	..	4 53	..	..	6 51	..	..	..		9 56
104½	Carmarthen ......arr	8 40	..		..	12 7	..	..		..	..	..	..	5 0	..	..	6 58	..	..	..		10 3
—	Llandilo ....dep	7 3	..	W.R. Train	9 17	1023	..	Saturdays only	W.R. Train	..	..	2 47	Except Saturdays	3 53	4 37	..	6 0	..	7 27	..	Saturdays only W.R. Train	9 4
91½	Ffairfach	..	..		9 20	..	..			..	..	2 50		..	4 41	..	..	..	7 30	..		..
93¾	Derwydd Road	..	..		9 28	..	..			..	..	3 7		..	4 48	..	..	..	7 43	..		..
95¼	Llandebie	..	..		9 32	..	..			..	..	3 11		..	4 52	..	..	..	7 47	..		..
97	Tirydail F	..	..		9 36	1639	..			..	..	3 15		4 8	4 56	..	..	..	7 51	..		9 19
97½	Parcyrhun Halt	..	..		9 39	..	..			..	..	3 18		..	4 59	..	..	..	7 54	..		..
98¾	Pantyffynnon .... arr	7 23	..		9 41	1044	..			..	..	3 20		4 13	5 1	..	6 18	..	7 56	..		..
	Pantyffynnon .... dep	7 24	..	8 29	9 43	1045	..		1244	..	..	3 22		4 14	5 4	..	6 20	..	8 0	..	9 5	..
103	Pontardulais, for Hendy arr	7 31	..	8 36	9 50	1052	..		1251	..	..	3 29		4 21	5 11	p.m	6 27	..	8 7	..	9 12	9 31
	Pontardulais, for Hendy dep	7 33	810	8 37	9 51	1055	..	1210	1252	1 0	1 54	3 30	3 45	4 23	5 12	5 28	6 30	6 40	8 9	8 33	9 13	9 33
106¾	Gorseinon G	7 40	818	Arr Llanelly 8 53 a.m	Arr Llanelly 10 8 a.m	11 2	..	1216	Arr Llanelly 1 8 p.m	1 6	2 0	Arr Llanelly 3 46 p.m	3 51	4 29	Arr Llanelly 5 28 p.m	5 34	..	6 46	Arr Llanelly 8 26 p.m	8 39	Arr Llanelly 9 30 p.m	9 39
108	Gowerton	7 44	822			11 6	..	1220		1 10	2 4		3 56	4 33		5 38	..	6 50		8 43		9 44
109¾	Dunvant	..	826			1110	..	1224		1 14	2 8		4 0	..		5 43	..	6 54		8 48		..
110¾	Killay	..	830			1114	..	1228		1 18	2 12		4 4	..		5 48	..	7 0		8 53		9P51
112½	Mumbles Road	7 54	834			1118	..	1232		1 22	2 16		4 10	4 43		5 53	6 47	7 5		8 58		9 58
114½	Swansea (Bay)	7 59	839			1124	..	1237		1 27	2 22		4 15	4 48		5 58	6 52	7 10		9 3		10 4
115¼	" (Vic) ...... arr	8 4	844			1129	..	1242		1 32	2 27		4 20	4 53		6 3	6 57	7 15		9 8		10 9

A Woodside
B Via Crewe
C 5 miles from Llanbister
D 4½ mils from Newbridge-on-Wye Sta.
F ½ mile to Ammanford
F Via Crewe. Does not apply on 25th September
G 1½ miles to Loughor
H Calls when required to take up

h Via Crewe. Dep. 11 40 a.m. on Saturdays
J Dep. 9 20 a.m. on Saturdays
K Via Crewe. Dep. 9 53 p.m. on Sundays
P Calls to set down from Craven Arms and beyond on notice being given to the Guard
p p.m.

T Through Carriage to Swansea (V.)
FC Through Carriages
U Fridays only
Z Night time

59.   A pre-grouping view of the station, fails to show that it was situated directly alongside the shore. It was photographed looking towards Swansea. (Lens of Sutton coll.)

60.   For the final part of the journey along the coast, the Central Wales Line ran alongside the Swansea & Mumbles Railway, also known as the Oystermouth Railway. One of the twin car double decker trams was captured as it was about to pass behind the station buildings on 10th September 1951. (H.C.Casserley)

61. The constant problem of sand being swept onto the tracks at this location was very apparent in this view of Stanier 2-6-2T no.40097 arriving at the station, with a train from Craven Arms in July 1955. (T.J.Edgington)

62. Two of the Mumbles tramcars are seen on 30th July 1958. The first station was replaced by the LNWR with one ¼ mile to the east on 2nd June 1892. (G.Adams/M.J.Stretton coll.)

63. During the last day of operation of the Mumbles line on 4th January 1960, another tramcar is seen passing behind the main line station. The location of the previous photograph was alongside the hotel situated on the road junction opposite the station buildings. (P.Kingston/R.S.Carpenter coll.)

64. More sand blown onto the tracks is evident in this view of the station looking east towards Swansea. Typical LNWR architecture and a characteristic footbridge are notable features in this view of 18th August 1963. (R.Patterson)

65.   During the final year of steam haulage on the route, Jubilee class 4-6-0s made an appearance on some of the through services. No.45577 *Bengal* was viewed awaiting departure from the station en route to Swansea during the August Bank Holiday weekend of 1963. (D.K.Jones coll.)

WEST OF SWANSEA

66.   Paxton Street was the principal locomotive depot for the Central Wales Line. Opened by the LNWR on 6th January 1882 (LMS code 4B), it became a sub-shed of Neath numbered 87K after nationalisation and was closed on 31st August 1959. Situated to the south of the main line, a short distance to the west of the terminal station, it had an allocation of 50 locomotives during its heyday. LNWR designed 0-8-4T no. 7941 was viewed at rest outside the shed on 17th September 1946.
(M.J.Stretton coll.)

67.   A fine array of former LMS motive power, featuring 4-6-0 no. 45298, 2-6-4T no.42388 and 0-6-0T no.47478, was being prepared for duty when photographed on 30th August 1955.   Following the closure of the depot, locomotives used on the CWL were obtained from other sheds in the area. This resulted in many of the former LMS types being replaced by BR Standard variants.
(E.H.Sawford/M.J.Stretton coll.)

68.   Class 8F no.48706 and BR class 3MT 2-6-2T no.82030 were viewed between duties during 1956. Note that the tank locomotive was equipped for "push-pull" operation. A decade later the 2-8-0 was destined to play a historic role when it hauled the last northbound train along the Somerset and Dorset route in March 1966. (D.K.Jones coll.)

69.   The principal express trains operating between Swansea and Shrewsbury were for many years invariably hauled by one of the magnificent class 5MT 4-6-0s, commonly known as "Black Fives". No.45422 was recorded prior to leaving the shed in 1957. (D.K.Jones coll.)

70.   The Fowler designed 2-6-4Ts of 1927 were a common sight on the CWL until the early 1960s. Surprisingly, very few of the later Stanier designed variations of the type were allocated to the route, the Fowlers being replaced by the BR 2-6-4Ts after 1961. No. 42390 was seen near the turntable during 1957. (D.K.Jones coll.)

71.   The first engine shed had been north of the running lines. A combination of former GWR and LMS locomotives are featured in this splendid view of the shed yard. Nos 8700, 48734, 5761 and 45143 are included, along with other residents of the later depot on 30th July 1958. (G.Adams/M.J.Stretton coll.)

72.   2-8-0 no.48452 was being steamed for duty at its home shed, shortly before the depot was closed in 1959. The superlative Stanier designed 8F locomotives were used for the haulage of heavy freight trains on the Central Wales Line for almost 30 years. Following their introduction in 1935, the 8Fs were to remain in action until the Swansea line closed in 1964. (P.Jones)

73.   This view of the gantry, with the No. 2 signal box in the distance, was recorded from a departing up train during 1962. The box closed on 14th June 1964. (A.M.Davies)

SWANSEA VICTORIA

XVI. The full extent of the railway network serving Swansea is on this 6ins to one mile survey of 1938. The LNWR route can be seen approaching from the coastal section bottom left, with Paxton Street Depot to the south of the main line. The former GWR connecting line between their station at High Street and South Dock is seen alongside the North Dock before passing to the east of Victoria Station at a higher level. As in so many urban locations, the prison was situated in close proximity to the railway.

74.   With rain streaming through the unglazed roof of the station, 2-6-4T no.42385 had just arrived at the buffer stops with a train from the north on 30th July 1958. (G.Adams/M.J.Stretton coll.)

75.   Two days later the weather conditions had improved as no.42385, with a fully loaded coal bunker, was seen about to depart from platform 2 with a local train to Llandovery. (G.Adams/ M.J.Stretton coll.)

42385

LOAD 2 TON

76. The glazed overall roof was badly damaged in an air-raid during World War II, and was destined to remain unglazed for the final two decades of the stations life. This 1961 view from the arrival platform shows the various huts that served as station facilities on the departure platform. The arches in the background carried the GWR connecting line to South Dock. (Lens of Sutton coll.)

77. This panoramic view of Swansea Victoria Station is from the embankment to the south of the running lines. No.3 signal box can be seen in the foreground, whilst class 5MT no.73036 was about to depart with the 18.25 "York Mail" on 15th September 1962. (R.Patterson)

78.   This view shows a BR class 5MT 4-6-0 prior to departure from platform 2, with a train bound for Shrewsbury in 1962. (D.Johnson/R.S.Carpenter coll.)

79.   One of the former GWR 0-6-0PTs is standing at the head of a rake of carriages in platform 1, prior to hauling them to the carriage shed during 1962. (D.Johnson/R.S.Carpenter coll.)

80.   The skeletal roof trusses framed this view of 4-6-0 no.45283 following its arrival at platform 1 on another wet day during 1962. This platform was partially protected from the elements by a section of roof that remained intact. (A.M.Davies)

81.   Class 5MT 4-6-0 no.73090 is blowing off excess steam in anticipation of its departure from platform 1, which was normally used for arrivals, with a train bound for Shrewsbury in 1962. (A.M.Davies)

82.   The fireman of the same locomotive was keeping a watchful eye on the platform activities prior to departure on the same occasion. The embankment carrying the GWR connecting line can be seen in the background. (A.M.Davies)

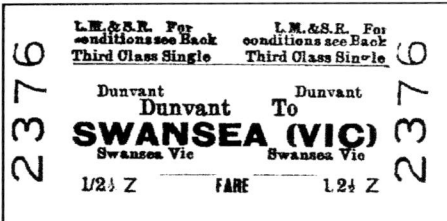

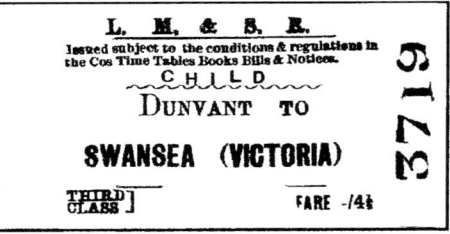

83.   Stanier 4-6-0 no.45283 from Shrewsbury shed was recorded as it was about to depart from platform 2, hauling the 9.40am service to its home station in August 1963. The GWR line can also be seen in this view. Goods traffic continued until 4th October 1965, trains using the line from the north. (D.K.Jones coll.)

84.   The exterior of the station was viewed on 20th September 1965, a year after it was closed. The section of the roof that escaped full impact of the wartime bombing mainly protected the administrative and parcels offices. (T.J.Edgington)

Llanelli Branch

PONTARDDULAIS

We now return to Pontarddulais in order to make a journey over the original section of the Llanelly Railway of 1839. This line has, of course, outlived the later LNWR direct line to Swansea Victoria, which closed in 1964. The junction between the two routes is shown on Map VIII.

85.   Our first view of what was then still a branch line features 0-6-0PT no.3719 arriving at the up platform with an early morning train from Llanelly on 29th April 1961. (R.M. Casserley)

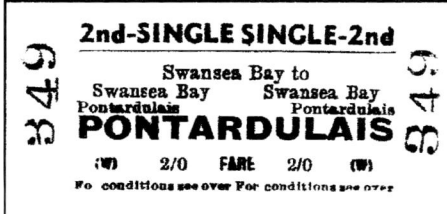

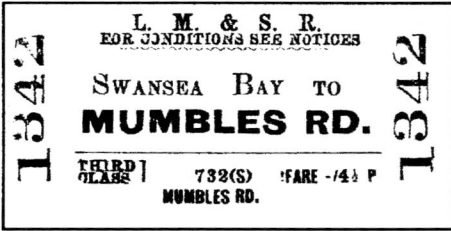

86.   Following the closure of the Swansea line in 1964, much of the station infrastructure was demolished and the line singled. This scene of desolation shows a DMU departing from the former platform 3 with a train bound for Llanelli during 1968. (WRRC / Stratton coll.)

87.   Single car unit no.153 323 was photographed on 27th September 2008 as it was about to cross the River Lougher heading towards Llanelli, amid the extensive tree growth that had overtaken much of the station area. (J.F.Organ)

88.   The bridge over the River Lougher was viewed on the same occasion. Part of the flood prevention scheme constructed in 1996 can be seen in the foreground. (J.F.Organ)

89.   The single bore 88 yard long tunnel constructed in 1838 is still serving its original purpose, as seen in 2008. The track through the tunnel was laid on concrete in 1983 in order to limit drainage problems.   (J.F.Organ)

HENDY AND MORLAIS JUNCTIONS

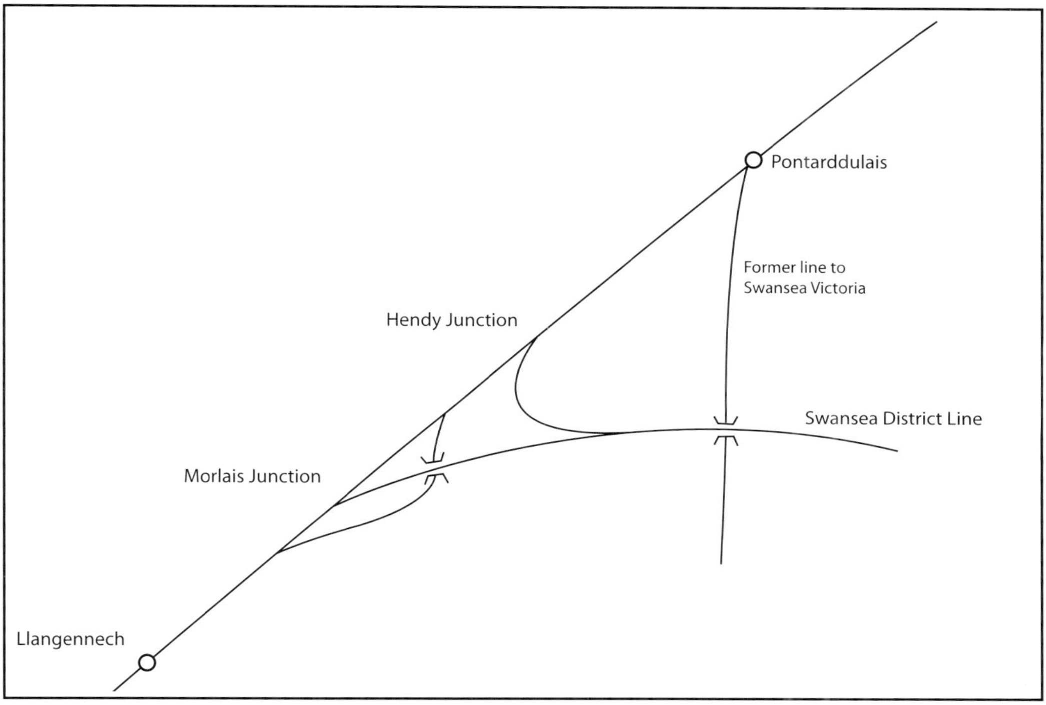

Pontarddulais

Former line to
Swansea Victoria

Hendy Junction

Swansea District Line

Morlais Junction

Llangennech

XVII. The triangular junction connecting the Central Wales Line to the Swansea District Line is featured. The original down line of the CWL passes under the southern arm of the triangle.

90.   Diesel locomotive no. 03 152 is seen at Hendy Junction whilst hauling a short freight train from Llandovery to Llanelli on 6th November 1981. The tracks in the foreground are those of the northern arm of the triangle. This area is now overshadowed by the M4 Motorway viaduct. (M.Hughes)

91.　　DMU no. C 812 is approaching Morlais Junction with a Shrewsbury to Swansea service, whilst a class 37 locomotive can be seen on the westbound tracks of the Swansea District Line. The former down line of the Central Wales route would have passed under the GWR tracks behind where the locomotive is standing. This scene was recorded on 12th July 1983.　(M.Hughes)

92.　　South of Morlais Junction, we witness a train, hauled by no. 37 296, heading south towards Llanelli, whilst no. 37 275 passes the photographer, bound for Pantyffynnon on 19th November 1982.　(M.Hughes)

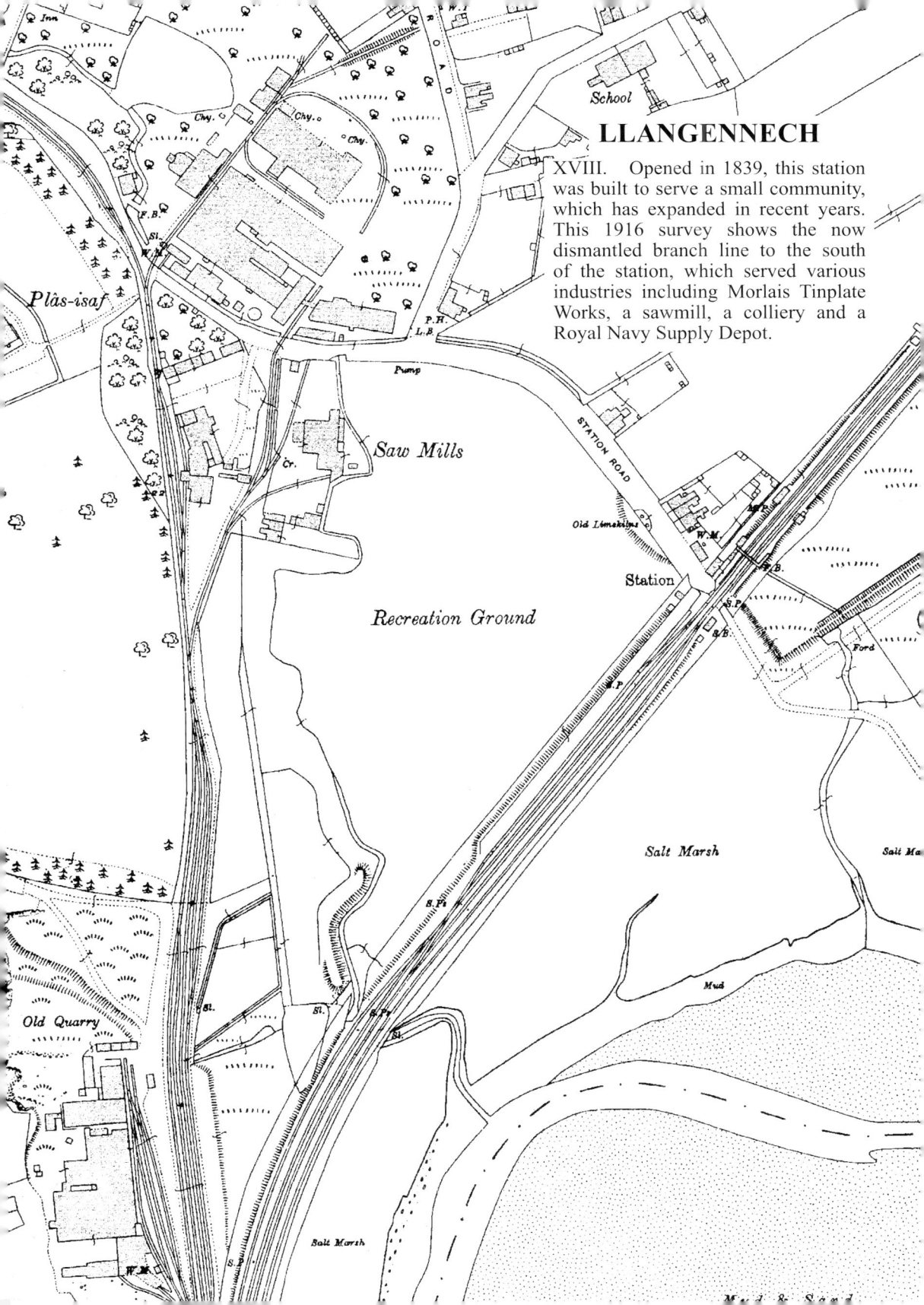

LLANGENNECH

XVIII. Opened in 1839, this station was built to serve a small community, which has expanded in recent years. This 1916 survey shows the now dismantled branch line to the south of the station, which served various industries including Morlais Tinplate Works, a sawmill, a colliery and a Royal Navy Supply Depot.

School

Inn

Plâs-isaf

Saw Mills

Pump

STATION ROAD

Old Limekilns

Station

Recreation Ground

Salt Marsh

Salt Ma

Mud

Ford

Old Quarry

Salt Marsh

93.   This view of the station looking north dates from 17th August 1982. Little changed subsequently. (F.A.Blencowe)

94.   On the same occasion, no. 37 223 was hauling a load of empty flat wagons towards Llanelli, when it was photographed south of the station. Local freight ceased on 12th July 1965 and the signal box closed on 21st November 1966. (F.A.Blencowe)

BYNEA

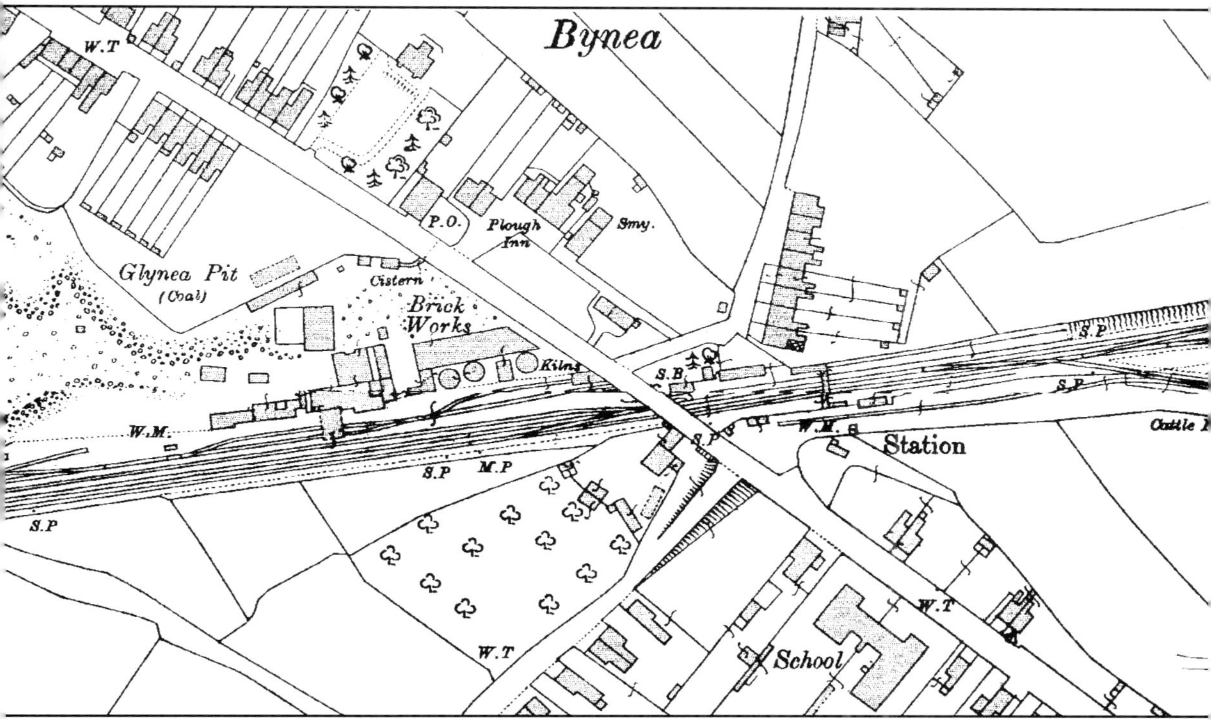

XIX.   This 1916 survey shows the once extensive station, located in close proximity to the brick works and Glynea Pit. The village is now absorbed into the suburbs of Llanelli. The term "Halt" was applied until May 1969.

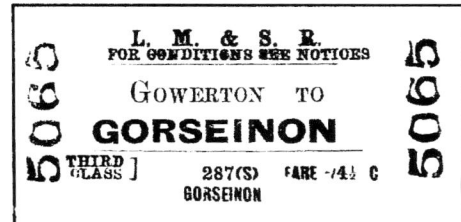

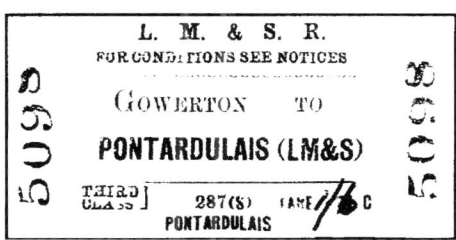

95.   This view of the station, looking towards Llanelli, was recorded during the 1950s. The station infrastructure was still complete on both platforms, along with the goods yard behind the down platform. The platforms appeared to be somewhat unkempt at that time. (R.K.Blencowe coll.)

96.   With recent housing development in the background, no. 37 205 hauls a long train of empty coal wagons bound for Pantyffynnon and passes the site of the former brick works on 9th September 1983. The goods yard closed on 12th July 1965 and the signal box followed on 21st November 1966. (M.Hughes)

LLANDEILO JUNCTION

97.   No. 47 079 was viewed as it was about to leave the Central Wales route at Llandeilo Junction, whilst hauling a load of empty coal wagons. This view was recorded on 30th March 1982. (F.A.Blencowe)

98.   A view in the opposite direction shows a DMU three car set leaving the Central Wales Line bound for Llanelli. The location of the former Llandilo Crossing would have been behind the photographer when this scene was captured on 20th August 1982. (F.A.Blencowe)

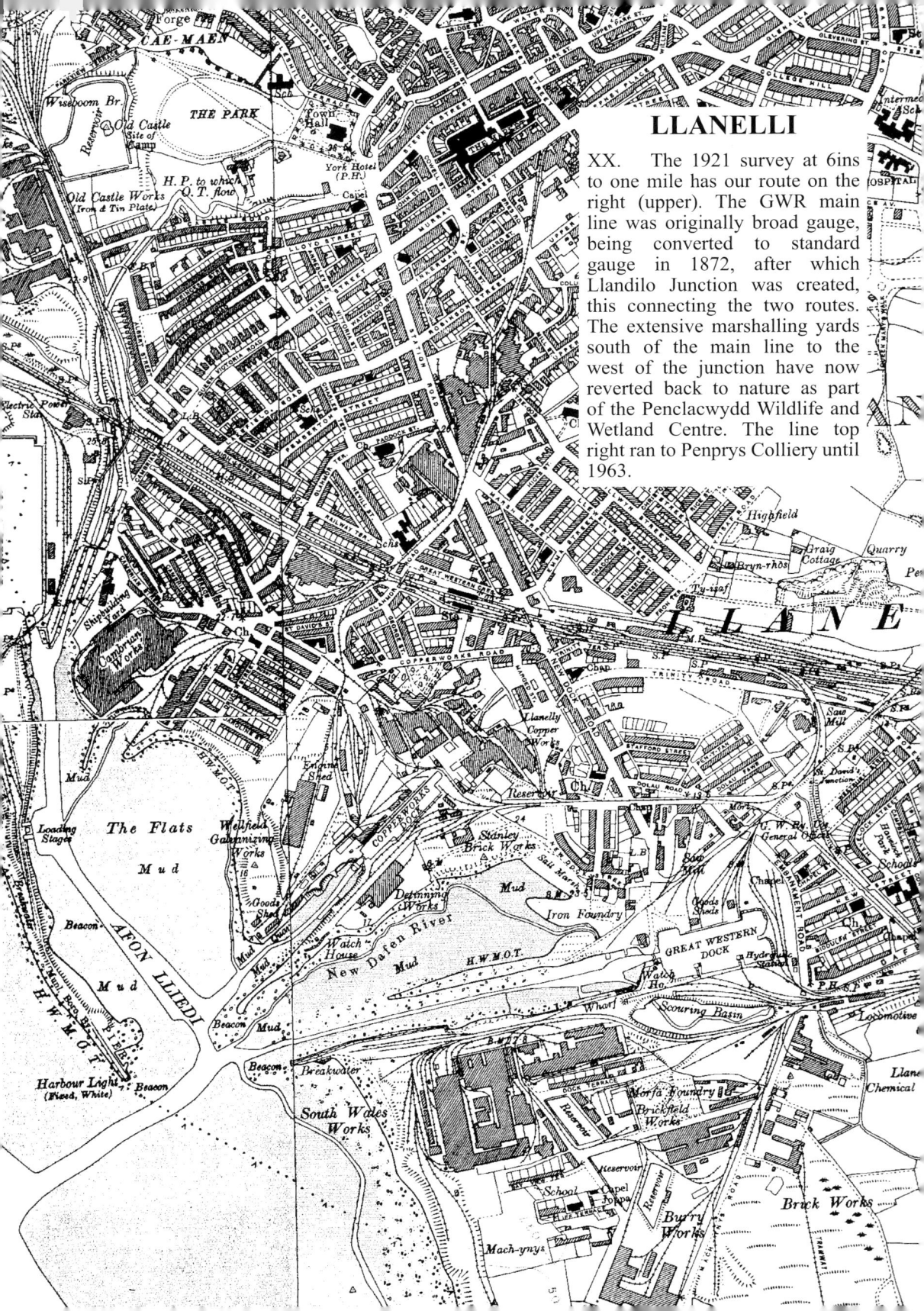

LLANELLI

XX.   The 1921 survey at 6ins to one mile has our route on the right (upper). The GWR main line was originally broad gauge, being converted to standard gauge in 1872, after which Llandilo Junction was created, this connecting the two routes. The extensive marshalling yards south of the main line to the west of the junction have now reverted back to nature as part of the Penclacwydd Wildlife and Wetland Centre. The line top right ran to Penprys Colliery until 1963.

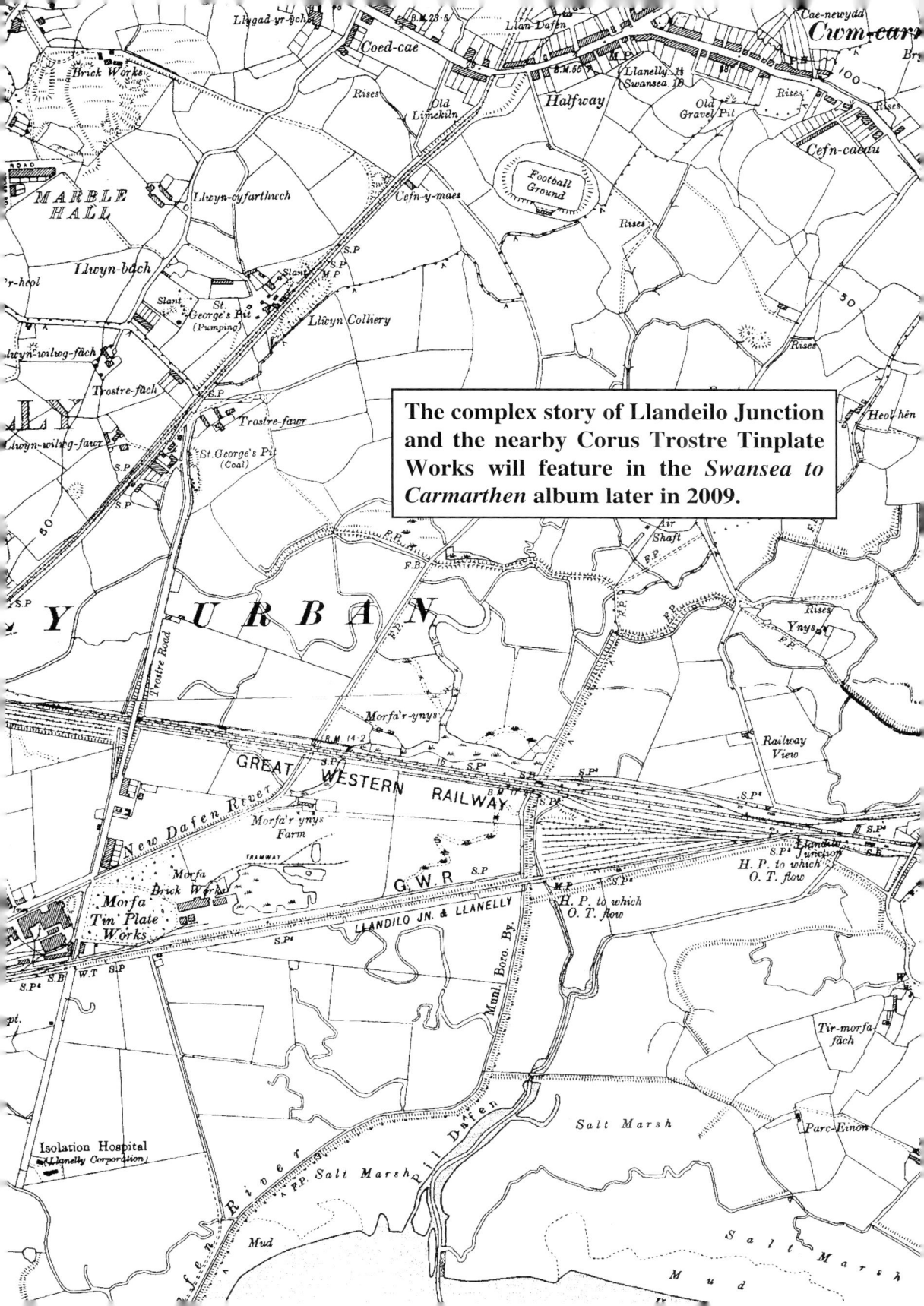

The complex story of Llandeilo Junction and the nearby Corus Trostre Tinplate Works will feature in the *Swansea to Carmarthen* album later in 2009.

99 This panoramic view of the station, looking from the west, is from the 1950s. On this occasion a solitary wagon was occupying the siding across the barrow crossing. (R.K.Blencowe coll.)

→ 100. Three years after the demise of steam in the area, this splendid water tank still stood to the west of station. The structure was photographed during 1967. Local goods traffic had ceased in 1965. (WRRC/Stratton coll.)

London & North Western Ry.

GOWERTON TO

PANTYFFYNNON

VIA PONTARDULAIS

Third] 287(S) [Class

PANTYFFYNNON

TURN OVER] FARE -/10

90 FE 28

1782

→ 101. DMU no. C800 was recorded as it departed towards Swansea High Street with a CWL train from Shrewsbury on 21st September 1985. (P.Jones)

102. Three car DMU set no. S945 had just arrived at the down platform when it was photographed on 16th September 1990. The train, known as the "Heart of Wales Rambler" ran from Swansea High Street to Llandrindod Wells. (M.J.Stretton)

103. The same train is seen departing from the station on the same occasion. This service was introduced by British Rail during the summer of 1990, prior to privatisation. (M.J.Stretton)

104. The station has retained much of its former GWR appearance, as seen in this view of the up platform in May 1996. (A.C.Mott)

105. A class 158 unit departs from the station with a train bound for Swansea. The former bay platform had disappeared beneath the vegetation and shrubs when this view was recorded during May 1998. (P.Jones)

Carmarthen Branch

We now retrace our route back to Llandeilo for a journey along the former LNWR branch line to Carmarthen. Originally opened as part of the Llanelly Railway and Dock Company system in 1864, it was transferred to the LNWR on 1st September 1873. It had already worked the line for two years. The 13 mile long route followed the River Towy for much of its journey between Carmarthen Valley Junction at Llandeilo and Abergwili Junction north of Carmarthen.

106.　0-6-0PT no.8777 was standing in the siding adjacent to the bay platform at Llandeilo with the stock of a train destined for Carmarthen when it was photographed on 1st August 1958. (G.Adams/M.J.Stretton coll.)

L. M. & S. R.
FOR CONDITIONS SEE NOTICES
GOLDEN GROVE TO
LLANDILO BRIDGE
THIRD CLASS]　992(S)　FARE -/5 C
LLANDILO B'DGE

8187 8187

LLANDILO BRIDGE

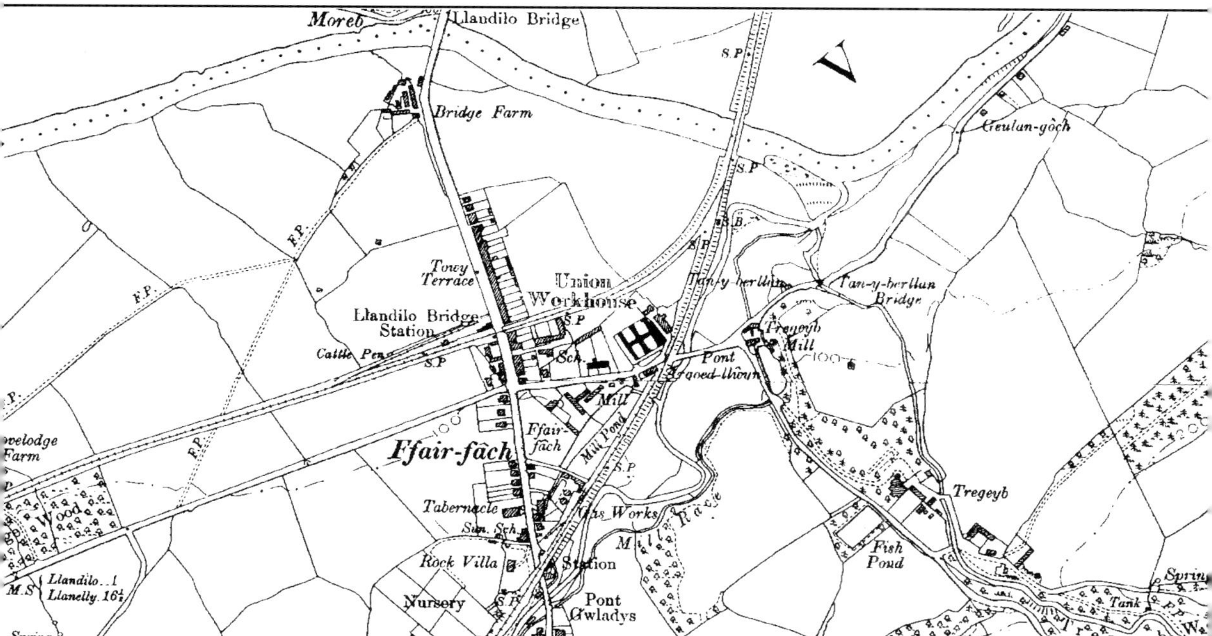

XXI. The 1907 survey clearly shows the branch diverging from the main line at the junction, immediately to the south of the bridge across the River Towy. The first station was situated to the north of Fairfach, a small community which benefited from being served by two stations.

107. This 1960 view of the station shows a typically rural setting with a single storey building gracing the platform and the level crossing beyond. The goods yard was open until the line closed in 1963. (Lens of Sutton coll.)

GOLDEN GROVE

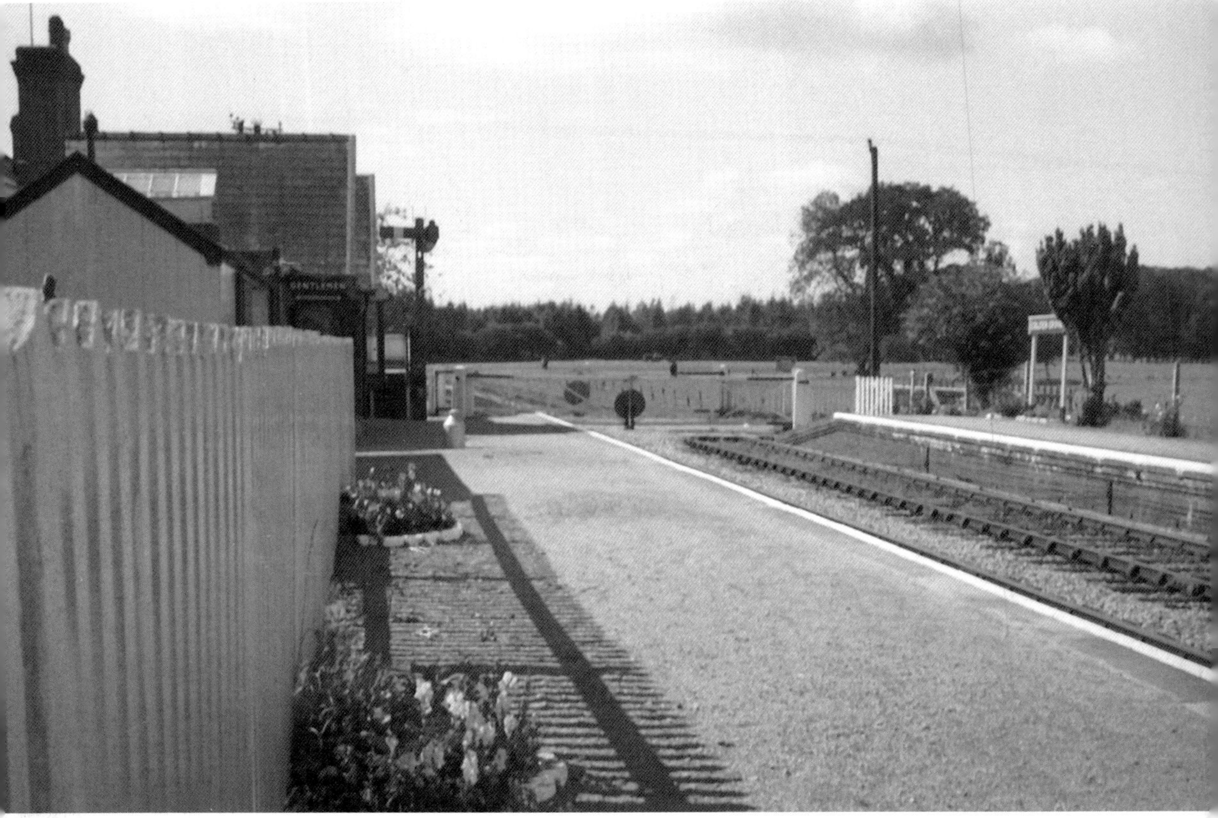

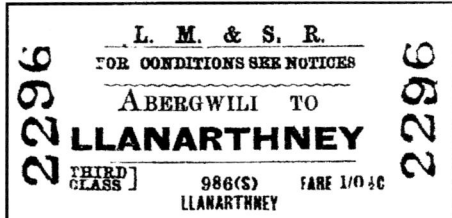

108. The delightfully named station featured a passing loop and with it the luxury of two platforms. This view was also recorded in 1960, and freight also lasted here to the end.
(Lens of Sutton coll.)

2296
L. M. & S. R.
FOR CONDITIONS SEE NOTICES
ABERGWILI TO
LLANARTHNEY
THIRD CLASS
986(S) FARE 1/0½C
LLANARTHNEY
2296

Gt. Western Ry. Gt. Western Ry
AMMANFORD AMMANFORD
TO Parly.(3rd Cls.)
CARMARTHEN
Via Llandilo and L. & N.W. Ry.
2/0 PARLY.[3rd Cls.] 2/0
Carmarthen Carmarthen
SE CK (H.G.)
078

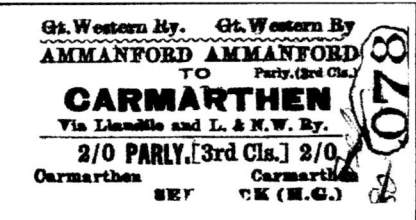

DRYSLLWYN

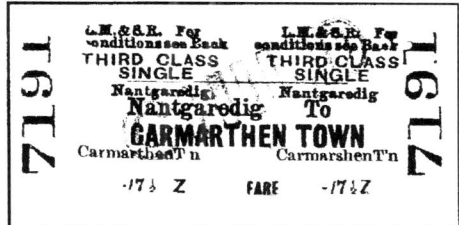

109. Perhaps better known for its castle, the name of which graces one of the surviving GWR express locomotives, this small station was provided with a small building of unique design as seen in this 1960 view. (Lens of Sutton coll.)

1184 2nd · SINGLE SINGLE · 2nd	7191 L.M.&S.R. Fg 7191 L.M.&S.R. Fg
Llandilo Bridge to	conditions see Back conditions see Back
Llandilo Bridge Llandilo Bridge	THIRD CLASS THIRD CLASS
Drysllwyn Drysllwyn	SINGLE SINGLE
DRYSLLWYN	Nantgaredig Nantgaredig
(W) 10d - Fare 10d (W)	Nantgaredig To
For conditions see over For conditions see over	**GARMARTHEN TOWN**
	Carmarthen T'n Carmarshen T'n
	·17½ Z FARE -17½ Z

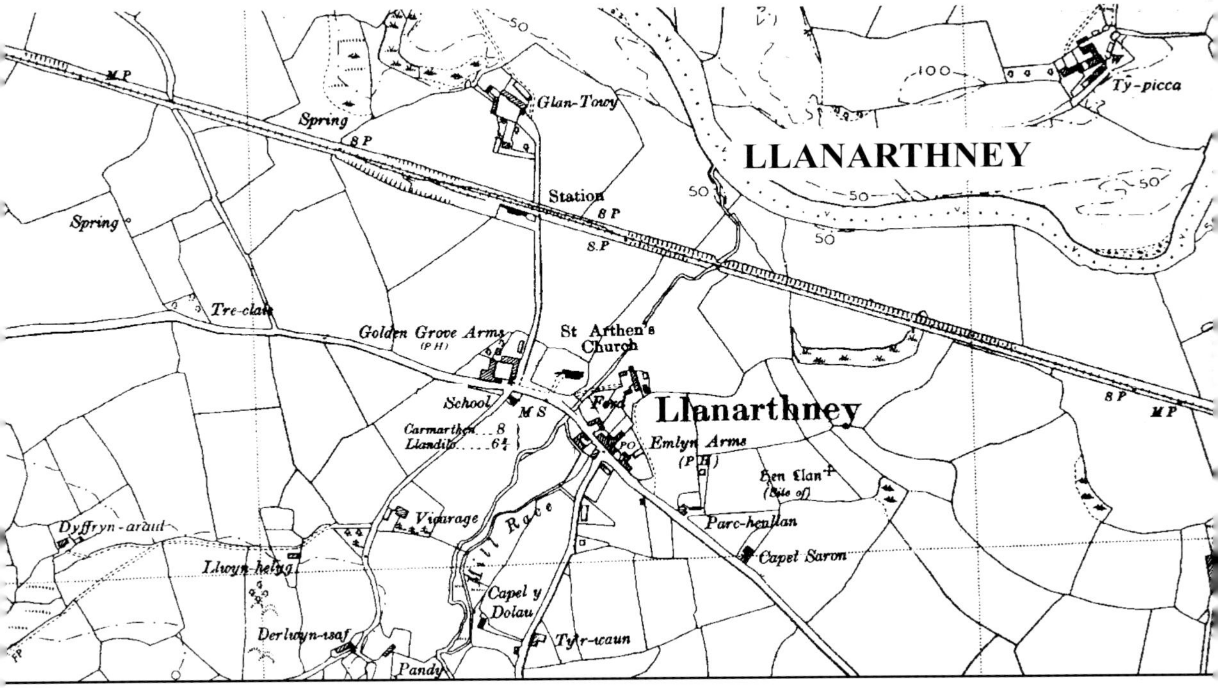

XXII. Situated between the village and the river, the small single platform station still had the benefit of a goods yard when surveyed in 1948. It closed on 1st June 1959.

110. The simple layout of the station was highlighted in this view looking towards Llandilo during the 1950s. A passing loop and a signal box existed here until 27th February 1938. (Lens of Sutton coll.)

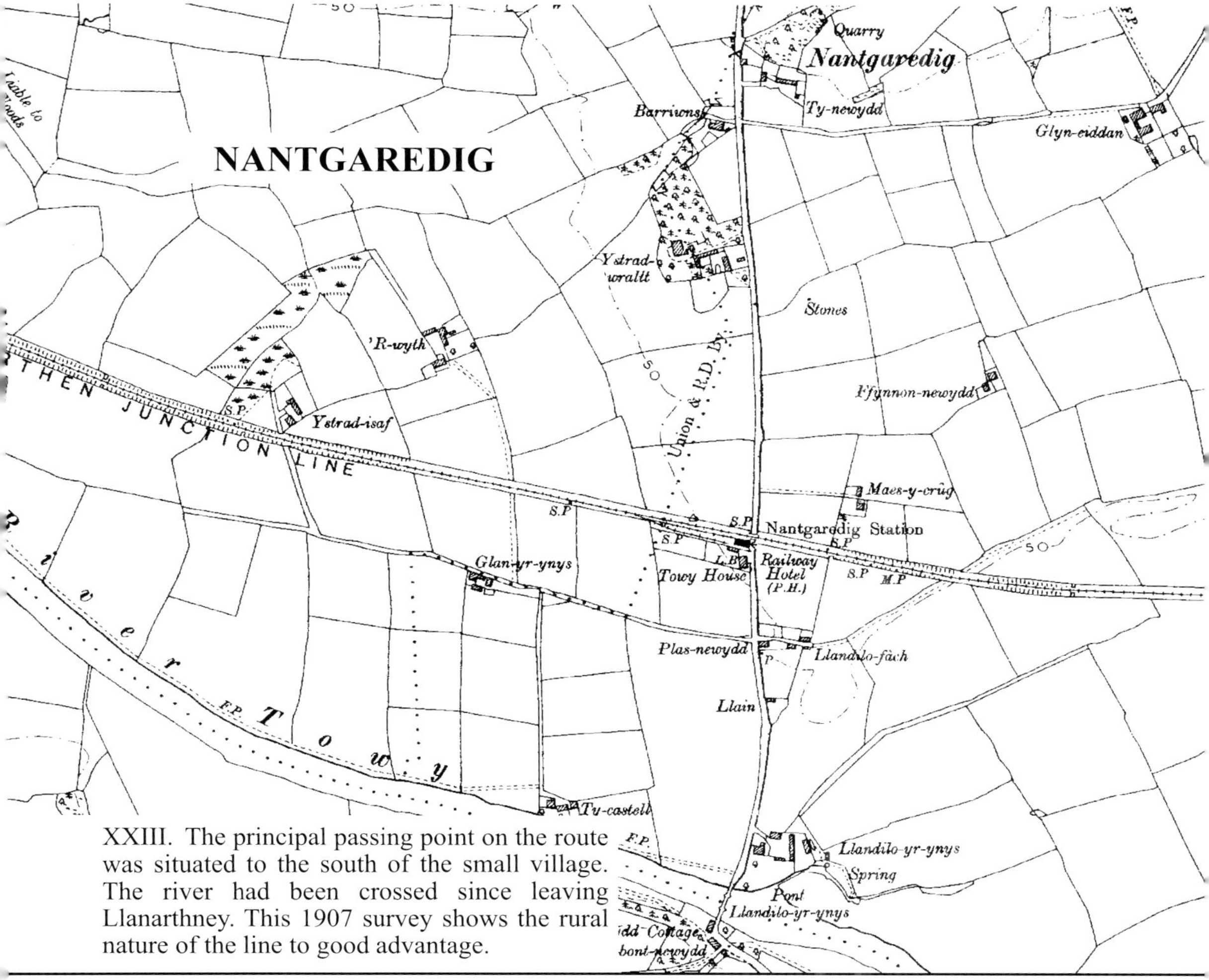

NANTGAREDIG

XXIII. The principal passing point on the route was situated to the south of the small village. The river had been crossed since leaving Llanarthney. This 1907 survey shows the rural nature of the line to good advantage.

111. This view of the station, looking towards Carmarthen, is from about 1912. The passing loop survived until the branch was closed in 1963. Carmarthenshire Farmers Co-operative Society had a siding from 1926 until 1963. (Lens of Sutton coll.)

112.   This view of the agricultural depot alongside the goods yard was recorded from a train bound for Llandilo during 1960. The depot was built in 1926 and consequently does not appear on the 1907 map. (A.M.Davies)

113.   This panorama looking east also shows the extensive layout of this country station, as it appeared in 1960. The goods depot closed with the line. (Lens of Sutton coll.)

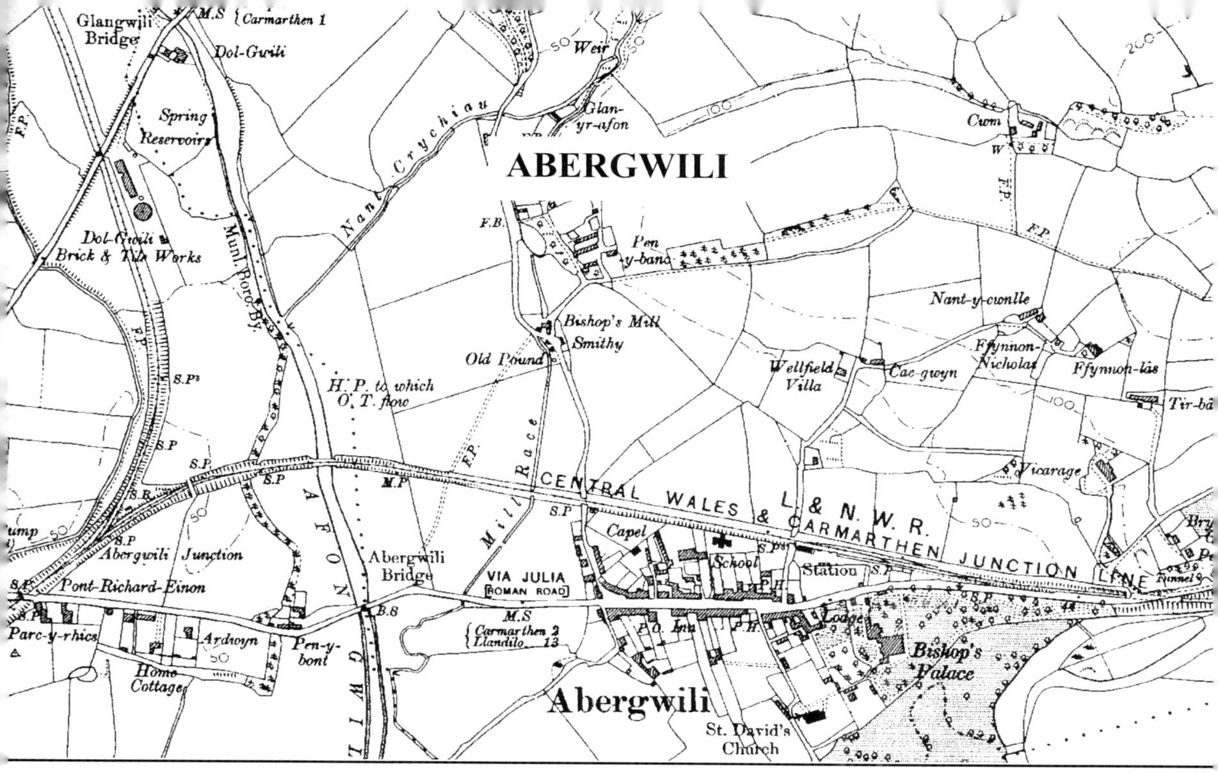

XXIV. The 1907 survey shows the station conveniently located near the village. The junction with the GWR line was situated one mile to the west, a short distance after the branch had crossed the River Gwili.

114.   The attractive presentation of the station, with its decorative gardens alongside the passing loop, was recorded in all its glory in around 1912. (Lens of Sutton coll.)

115. This view of the station looking towards Carmarthen, shows the platform and the goods bay alongside during 1960. Everything looks neat and tidy, despite the fact that closure was looming, even the remnants of the gardens are still visible. (Lens of Sutton coll.)

ABERGWILI JUNCTION

116. 0-6-0PT no.7444 was recorded as it joined the GWR route at the junction on 2nd August 1963, with a train from Llandilo shortly before the branch was closed. The GWR route, which was also shortly destined for closure, ran from Carmarthen to Aberystwyth by a scenic route. (E.Wilmshurst)

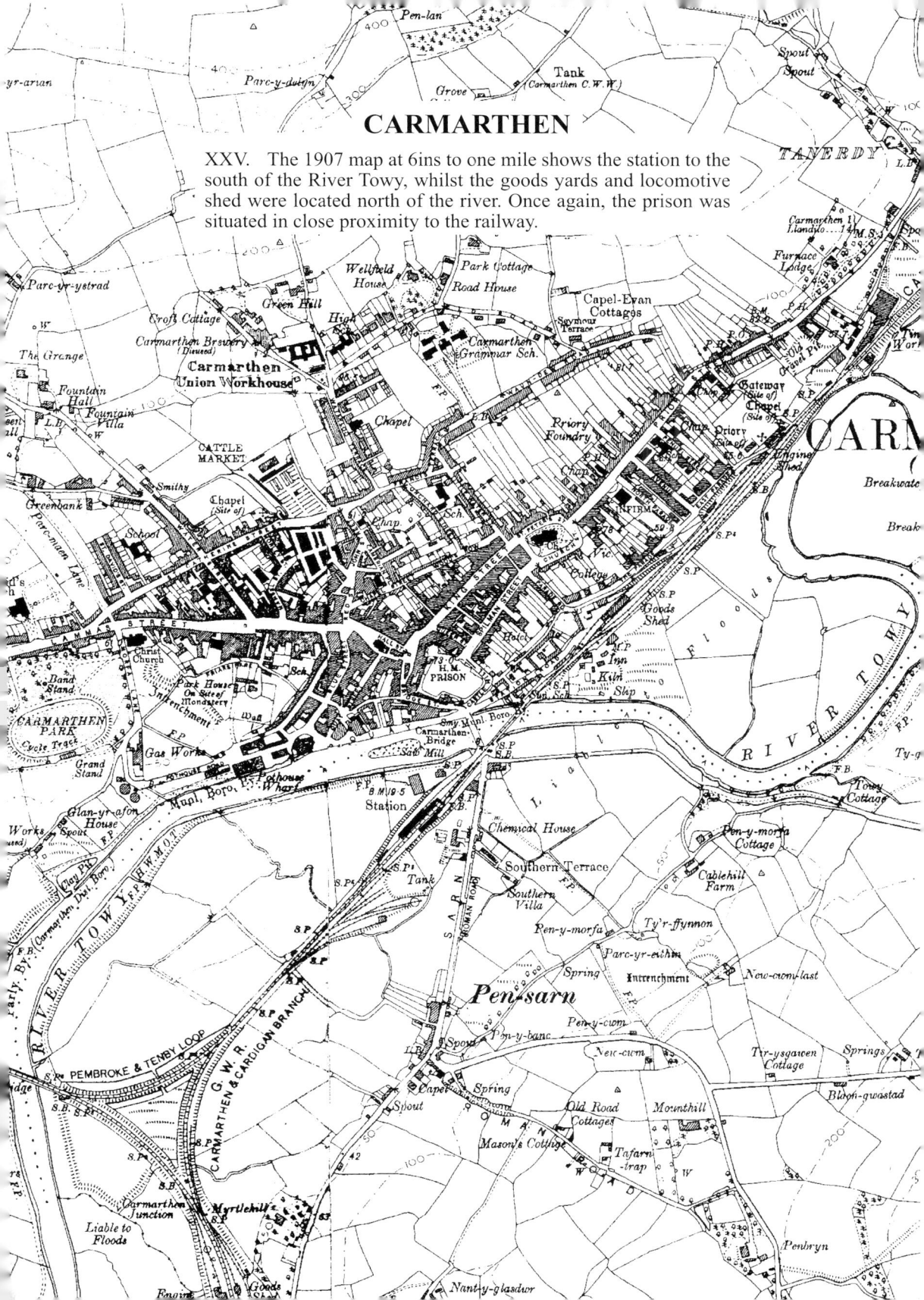

CARMARTHEN

XXV. The 1907 map at 6ins to one mile shows the station to the south of the River Towy, whilst the goods yards and locomotive shed were located north of the river. Once again, the prison was situated in close proximity to the railway.

117.   Former LMS 0-6-2T no. 6757, one of the illustrious LNWR "Coal Tanks" designed by Francis Webb in 1882, was viewed passing the signal box to the south of the river bridge on 16th August 1935. (H.F.Wheeller/R.S.Carpenter coll.)

118.   This panoramic view, looking south, shows the site of the former LNWR locomotive depot in the foreground. The scene was recorded on 21st September 1962, 12 months before the branch to Llandilo closed. (R.S.Carpenter)

119.   No. 33 020 is seen crossing the bridge across the River Towy on the remaining stub of the Aberystwyth and Llandeilo lines, with no.37 218 in the distance. The bridge was demolished a short time after this view was obtained on 27th September 1982. (P.Jones)

120.   The station is now a terminus at the head of the triangular junction connected to the main line linking Swansea and Fishguard. No.33 020 was photographed as it was due to depart with a train bound for Swansea on the same day as the previous illustration. (P.Jones)

MP Middleton Press

EVOLVING THE ULTIMATE RAIL ENCYCLOPEDIA

Easebourne Lane, Midhurst, West Sussex.
GU29 9AZ Tel:01730 813169

www.middletonpress.co.uk   email:info@middletonpress.co.uk
A-978 0 906520   B- 978 1 873793   C- 978 1 901706   D-978 1 904474   E - 978 1 906008

OOP Out of print at time of printing - Please check availability   BROCHURE AVAILABLE SHOWING NEW TITLES